Ministry
Information Centre, 13th Floor,
Mowat Block, Queen's Park,
Toronto, Ont.   M7A 1L2

IMPLEMENTING RACE AND ETHNOCULTURAL EQUITY POLICY IN ONTARIO SCHOOL BOARDS

KAREN R. MOCK, Principal Investigator
VANDRA L. MASEMANN

This research project was funded under contract by the Ministry of Education, Ontario.

It reflects the views of the authors and not necessarily those of the Ministry.

Sean Conway, Minister
Bernard J. Shapiro, Deputy Minister

© QUEEN'S PRINTER FOR ONTARIO, 1990

Order Information:

MGS Publications Services
880 Bay Street, 5th Floor
Toronto, Ontario
M7A 1N8
(416) 965-6015
(Toll Free) 1-800-268-7540
(Toll Free from area code 807,
ask operator for Zenith 67200).

Order must be accompanied by a
cheque or money order payable
to the Treasurer of Ontario

Canadian Cataloguing in Publication Data

```
Mock, Karen R., 1945-
  Implementing race and ethnocultural equity policy
in Ontario school boards

Includes bibliographical references.
ISBN 0-7729-6197-2

1. Educational equalization--Ontario.  2. Minorities--
Education--Ontario.  I. Masemann, Vandra L., 1944- .
II. Ontario. Ministry of Education.  III. Title.

LC213.3.C3206   1989    370.19'342'09713   C89-099666-0
```

TABLE OF CONTENTS

LIST OF TABLES	v
LIST OF FIGURES	vi
ACKNOWLEDGEMENTS	vii
ABSTRACT	viii
EXECUTIVE SUMMARY	x
INTRODUCTION	1
BACKGROUND AND PURPOSE OF THE STUDY	3
METHOD	6
RESULTS	8
POLICIES AND DOCUMENTS ON RACE AND ETHNOCULTURAL EQUITY	8
QUESTIONNAIRE ON RACIAL AND ETHNOCULTURAL EQUITY	18
Francophone Issues	42
Aboriginal Issues	46
INTERVIEWS ON POLICY DEVELOPMENT AND IMPLEMENTATION	50
SUMMARY AND CONCLUSIONS	59
RECOMMENDATIONS FOR ACTION	63
RESOURCE BIBLIOGRAPHY	67
APPENDIX A: LISTS OF BOARDS THAT PARTICIPATED IN THIS STUDY	82
A1: ALPHABETICAL LIST OF BOARDS IN SURVEY I	83
A2: ALPHABETICAL LIST OF BOARDS THAT HAVE AN OVERALL POLICY	84
A3: ALPHABETICAL LIST OF BOARDS THAT ARE DEVELOPING A POLICY	85
A4: ALPHABETICAL LIST OF BOARDS THAT DO NOT HAVE AN OVERALL POLICY	86
APPENDIX B: RESEARCH TOOLS	87
B1: SURVEY I LETTER	88
B2: SURVEY II LETTER AND QUESTIONNAIRE (ENGLISH)	89
B3: SURVEY II LETTER AND QUESTIONNAIRE (FRENCH)	96
B4: INTERVIEW PROTOCOL	102
B5: FOLLOW-UP LETTER AND FORM	104
B6: LETTER OF THANKS	106

LIST OF TABLES

TABLE 1: OVERVIEW OF SCHOOL BOARD POLICIES	10
TABLE 2: BOARDS WITH POLICIES BY REGION	19
TABLE 3: BOARDS DEVELOPING A POLICY BY REGION	20
TABLE 4: BOARDS WITH NO OVERALL POLICY BY REGION	21
TABLE 5: BOARDS WITH AND WITHOUT POLICIES WHICH HAVE DOCUMENTS IN OTHER AREAS	23
TABLE 6: PARTICIPATION IN VALIDATION OF MINISTRY DOCUMENT BY BOARDS WITH A POLICY AND BOARDS WITHOUT A POLICY	26
TABLE 7: FOLLOW-UP TO THE VALIDATION PROCESS IN ORDER OF FREQUENCY	26
TABLE 8: STAGE OF POLICY DEVELOPMENT BY BOARDS WITH AND WITHOUT POLICY	29
TABLE 9: THE MAIN RACIAL AND ETHNOCULTURAL MINORITY GROUPS (IN ORDER OF MAGNITUDE)	29
TABLE 10: FOUR MAIN MINORITY GROUPS BY BOARDS WITH OR WITHOUT POLICY	31
TABLE 11: THE PROCESS AND PERSONNEL INVOLVED IN POLICY DEVELOPMENT AND IMPLEMENTATION	31
TABLE 12: FACTORS WHICH LED TO SUCCESS IN THE DEVELOPMENT OF POLICY	33
TABLE 13: MAIN FACTORS THAT PREVENT SUCCESS OR ARE A BARRIER TO POLICY DEVELOPMENT (LISTED BY FREQUENCY)	36
TABLE 14: UNIQUE FACTORS TO BE TAKEN INTO CONSIDERATION WITH REGARDS TO POLICY DEVELOPMENT (LISTED BY FREQUENCY)	37
TABLE 15: LOCAL RESOURCES FOR POLICY DEVELOPMENT OR PROFESSIONAL DEVELOPMENT DAYS	39
TABLE 16: BOARD'S HIGHEST PRIORITY IN NEXT FIVE YEARS	40

LIST OF FIGURES

FIGURE 1: PERCENTAGES OF BOARDS WITH AND WITHOUT POLICIES WITH DOCUMENTATION IN OTHER AREAS 19

FIGURE 2: PERCEPTIONS OF LEVEL OF POLICY DEVELOPMENT BY BOARDS WITH AND WITHOUT OVERALL POLICIES 20

ACKNOWLEDGEMENTS

We would like to thank all of the school boards that participated in this study and all of the school personnel and community members who spoke to us in interviews. We also greatly appreciate the assistance of the Regional Race Relations Officers of the Ministry of Education.

We also wish to acknowledge Brenda Deshane for her assistance in document processing and initial data analysis. We are grateful to our research associate, Jacinthe Fraser, for conducting the francophone component of the study and special thanks are due to Althea Rhooms for her research assistance and tireless contribution to the final stages of the project. Thank you also to Lynn Knowles for her assistance in the production of the report.

ABSTRACT

This report presents the results of a survey of all school boards in Ontario to determine whether or not they have policies for race and ethnocultural equity and, if so, to what extent they are being implemented at the present time.

Of the 124 boards contacted, 100 responded in some way by submitting copies of their policies and support documents, completing a questionnaire, and/or agreeing to be interviewed to provide insights into the processes of policy development and implementation in this area.

The major findings of this study are as follows:

1. There are 39 boards with race and ethnocultural equity policies and 3 other boards have completed drafts of policies. Twenty-two (22) boards have begun a process of policy development and are proceeding in this direction.

2. The size, structure, content, and format of the policies vary widely, from one page of policy statements to 40 pages of policy and accompanying administrative procedures.

3. Boards with race and ethnocultural equity policies usually have related policies and/or documents, such as multiculturalism, heritage language, employment equity, racial harassment, and curriculum guidelines or have included these areas as components of their race and ethnocultural equity policies. Boards without an overall policy have fewer policies or documents in related areas.

4. A small number of northern rural boards have managed to utilize limited resources to develop policies. However, in general, boards with race and ethnocultural equity or related policies tend to be larger urban southern boards with greater access to resources.

5. The **key factors in** success of policy development and implementation were identified as:
    - attitude, support and commitment of senior administrators
    - political will of the decision makers

- recognition that racism exists and a desire to eradicate it from our school systems
- adequate internal and external resources
- community involvement for input, validation and monitoring
- responsibility and accountability clearly outlined in the policy and procedures
- effective in-service training at all levels of the system

6. Boards are looking to the Ministry of Education to provide leadership and modelling for policy development and implementation by mandating policy and by providing both financial and human resources and guidelines for boards in keeping with their needs and situations.

Specific issues are highlighted for boards serving large francophone and native populations. Recommendations for action based on the research findings conclude the report, with a view towards achieving race and ethnocultural equity in education across Ontario. A selected bibliography of primarily Canadian research and resources is included.

EXECUTIVE SUMMARY

A survey was conducted of all 124 school boards in the Province of Ontario in order to determine which boards have policies for race and ethnocultural equity and to what extent and with what success those policies are being implemented, and to identify the key factors in success and/or barriers to effective policy development and implementation in this area. Letters were sent to the director of education in each board, requesting that she or he submit copies of the policy and related documents. A questionnaire followed the initial letter, and relevant board personnel provided responses that gave insights into the process of policy development and the current stage of implementation. Directors were asked to identify contact persons who could be contacted and interviewed to give further information.

Broad Data Base

Of the 124 boards contacted, 100 responded within the time frame (March - May, 1989) by submitting copies of their policies and support documents, completing the questionnaire, and/or agreeing to be interviewed. This high response rate (80.6%) provides a reliable overview of the "state of the art" of race and ethnocultural equity policy development and implementation in school boards across the province. In addition to the 100 written responses, interviews were conducted personally or by telephone with 43 contact people representing 22 school boards in 10 cities. Visits were made to Windsor, Hamilton, London, Ottawa, Timmins, Parry Sound, and Waterloo, in addition to those interviews conducted in selected boards in Metropolitan Toronto.

Policies in Ontario

It was found that 39 school boards have policies on race and ethnocultural equity or closely related areas (i.e., multiculturalism and race relations or multicultural, ethnic and race relations) and 3 other boards have drafts of such policies that are in the final stages of validation.

Copies of these policies and related documents (e.g., brochures, curriculum materials, pamphlets, board newsletters on race and ethnocultural equity) are on file in the office of the deputy minister's special advisor on race relations and plans are underway for making these materials available to school boards that could benefit from the extensive work done by several boards in this field.

It is significant to note that an additional 22 boards have begun the process of policy development for race and ethnocultural equity and are at varying stages in this process. It was found that the size, structure, content, and format of the policies vary widely, from one page to approximately 40 pages, including detailed administrative procedures. The latter type seem to lead to more effective implementation plans and practices.

In terms of additional documentation, it was found that boards with policies in race and ethnocultural equity are far more likely to have related policies and/or materials and documents than boards without an overall policy.

Policy Development and Implementation

Policies dealing with race and ethnocultural equity are considered to be different from other policies because of the nature of their content and pervasiveness of outcomes. In general, the **major findings** are as follows:

- 39 boards have policies, 3 have drafts that are nearly completed, and over 20 boards are in the process of developing a policy;

- these policies are considered to be different from other policies because of the nature of their content and pervasiveness of outcomes;

- they take longer to develop than other policies (average 18 months to 2 years);

- they usually involve community input, validation and monitoring;

- the entire system is (or should be) affected by these policies;

- there is often tremendous resistance to overcome in policy development and implementation: this resistance may be obvious or covert;

- responsibility and accountability must be built into the policy to ensure implementation;

- staff responsible for these policies are often vulnerable, must take risks, and need real and moral support to reduce stress and enhance efficiency;

- francophone school boards and francophone sections of school boards are at the beginning of the process of policy development in race and ethnocultural equity. Their situation is more complex than that of anglophone school boards because of their historical position, the cultural/heterogeneity of the francophone population of Ontario, and the racial diversity of French-speaking immigrants to Canada;

- several school boards in the province have created policies that have effectively acknowledged the concerns of native parents and students, particularly in curriculum and guidance; however, many school boards have not yet perceived that the needs of native students should be addressed in a policy of race and ethnocultural equity;

- school boards feel they need additional financial and human resources or resource allocation to develop and implement policies in this area;

- there are useful resources and resource people available throughout the province, but knowledge about them needs to be disseminated and shared through networking and funding;

- the content, format, structure and language of policies vary widely and will have to be standardized somewhat to ensure equity for all Ontarians, but appropriate for specific areas and needs;

- in-service training is viewed as essential for all staff, trustees, and committee members to enhance policy development and implementation.

Recommendations

The results of the survey and interviews across the province suggest the following recommendations for action:

1. In order for the development and implementation of policies and procedures for race and ethnocultural equity to become a priority among school boards, the ministry should make such policies **mandatory**, including responsibilities and accountability.

2. Clear **guidelines** for policy development and implementation should be made available, and sufficient resources allocated to enable all boards to develop and implement policies effectively, according to provincial standards and also according to their particular needs and context.

3. **Information** on existing policies and support documents should be made available in a format that is easily accessible to every board in the province.

4. Local **resource** centres should be set up by the ministry in each region to provide a clearinghouse of information, specialized resource collections, and local speakers and resource persons for workshops, committees and task forces.

5. The Ministry of Education should assist the regions in setting up **networks** of personnel involved in policy development and implementation, to share information and resources and provide the outside support necessary for effective work in this area.

6. A **policy development manual** should be developed, based on the results of this study, to present various models of policy development and practical step-by-step guidelines on implementation. Sections should be included on francophone and native issues and how to involve the community effectively.

7. The Government of Ontario should **allocate funds** to enable the Ministry of Education to assist boards of education through a system of grants to develop policy and implementation procedures since effective policy

development requires sufficient time and the commitment (and release time) of various staff members, as well as a level of support for the process that can put a strain on smaller boards with fewer resources.

8. Funds should be made available to conduct **research** on the efficacy of policy and procedures in effecting change in social attitudes and behaviour in children in schools, as well as research on employment practices in school boards.

9. Since many boards of education are looking to the **Ministry of Education** for leadership and guidance in this area, the basic tenets of race and ethnocultural equity should be practiced by the ministry itself. That is, the ministry should conduct a review of internal policies, practice, and programs within its purview with a view to developing and implementing procedures to achieve race and ethnocultural equity. These would include:

- enhancing the **curriculum** of all ministry courses (especially those for supervisory officers and principals) to include adequate preparation in this area;

- developing **employment policies** and procedures to eliminate barriers to equality in employment within the ministry;

- providing **in-service training** to all ministry personnel to enhance their awareness, understanding and skills in managing and valuing diversity;

- providing intensive training to all **education officers** with responsibilities for race relations, so that they can provide resources, leadership, and guidance in the regions;

- establishing criteria **for evaluation** and monitoring of policy development and implementation;

- **funding research** and providing incentives both in the ministry and in school boards to determine the effectiveness of policy development in effecting change in all areas addressed by the policies;

- including knowldege and experience in race and ethnocultural equity issues as **requirements for teacher** certification in the Province of Ontario.

10. In the carrying out of all the above recommendations, particular attention should be paid to the interests and concerns of school boards serving **native** and **francophone** populations.

INTRODUCTION

The issues of race and ethnocultural equity have been a concern of the Government of Ontario for a considerable period of time. The Government's Race Relations Policy, passed in 1985, clearly enunciates the principles underlying race and ethnocultural equity. The earlier Multicultural Policy passed in 1977, also acknowledges the diverse nature of Ontario society and the rights and responsibilities of its citizens of diverse backgrounds. The Ontario Human Rights Commission was established to uphold these and other rights. Ultimately, the Canadian Charter of Rights and Freedoms enshrines these rights and Clause 27 of the Constitution states that all constitutional provisions shall be interpreted within a multicultural framework.

In Ontario, the Ministry of Education has a mandate to educate children from Junior Kindergarten to Grade 13 and also adults, all within the framework of race and ethnocultural equity. The Government's pay equity legislation, which is to be put into practice by 1990, also affects how school boards deal with contractual negotiations for employment by teachers' unions and other employee groups. The publications of guidelines for publishers and authors on bias in educational materials also takes these principles into the curriculum materials used every day in the classroom. The acknowledgement of gender inequities, the establishment of French-speaking schools, and the provision of programs for aboriginal students also exist within a framework of equity and language rights. The extension of provincial funding to separate schools has added a new dimension to the equation. Overall, the situation in Ontario has changed in the 1980s as new legislation and constitutional provisions have been aimed at creating equality and social justice for all citizens.

The change in climate in the 1980s has provided a better legislative base for equity, at the same time as other social forces such as movement to the cities, dramatic increases in the cost of housing, conflicts over use of forests in Northern Ontario, increased homelessness among school-aged children, increased use of drugs, and confrontation with police have produced more overt examples of racial and ethnocultural tension and conflict. Thus the impetus to develop strategies to achieve race and ethnocultural equity can be viewed from a perspective of conflict and this perception has had a profound effect on policy makers at the school board level. Past efforts at multicultural policy development were couched in terms of social harmony, ethnic identity, and understanding, a stance often decried by critics of "song and dance" multiculturalism. As will be shown in this report, the anticipated outcomes of multicultural and race relations policies may be similar; or they may be quite different. For example, one measure of "success" of policies concerning racial harassment is a change in the number of incidents reported. On the other hand, the measures of "success" of a multicultural policy usually refer to attitude change, enriched curriculum, improved school-community relations, and so on. However, multicultural policies have often been critized for failing to "address problems rooted not in cultural differences but in racial inequities of power and privilege". (*The Development of a Policy on Race and Ethnocultural Equity, Report of the Provincial Advisory Committee*, 1987, p. 38).

The scope of race and ethnocultural equity policy is thus to address racism and discrimination at their roots, to acknowledge conflict, and to deal with it. The Report of the Provincial Advisory Committee referred to above lists the prime objectives of an equity policy as noted are as follows:

- to define, isolate, and eliminate racism and discriminatory policies (and practices);

- to challenge prejudice and discrimination;

- to build upon the strengths of Ontario's cultural and racial diversity;

- to ensure equality of opportunity for all students preparing to live and work harmoniously in Canada or any other society;

- to promote an environment that treats students, staff, and school communities fairly and justly, acknowledging and respecting their racial and ethnocultural background;

- to meet the needs of all people with due regard to their race, ethnicity, culture, language, gender, and religion (*ibid*., p.4)

BACKGROUND AND PURPOSE OF THE STUDY

In the last decade, several school boards have taken initiatives to respond to the changing populations in their areas, and to address such issues as multiculturalism, heritage languages, English as a second language, and more recently, race relations. Although in the 1970s there appeared to be widespread acceptance of the concept of multiculturalism in education and the value of recognizing and celebrating the contribution of Canadians of **all** racial and ethnocultural backgrounds, several incidents that occurred in school boards in the late 1970s and early 1980s pointed out the need to have effective race relations policies in place to prevent discrimination against individuals and groups that result in inequalities in both education and employment, and to give school board personnel (staff and students) the awareness and ability to respond effectively when such incidents do occur.

In response to the growing need for policy and resources in this area, the Ministry of Education took steps to move towards change. In March 1986 the ministry co-sponsored a conference on race and ethnocultural relations with the Ministry of Citizenship and Culture (something now referred to as the joint conference). This was attended by approximately 10 representatives from every board across the province, including trustees, directors, superintendents, and persons charged with responsibilities in the area of multiculturalism and race relations. In addition to workshops covering a wide range of topics, a document was introduced entitled "Towards a Policy" that had been prepared as a generic policy model by a committee of educators and consultants under the asupices of the Race Relations Division of the Ontario Human Rights Commission, Ministry of Labour. The Ministry of Education responded by creating the Provincial Advisory Committee on Race Relations to work on a document specific to education. In addition to the education officer responsible for multiculturalism, a race relations position was created to staff the advisory committee and prepare resource documents.

A report on the joint conference and an accompanying Inventory of Resource Persons (who could assist boards with race and ethnocultural equity policy development and in-service training programs) were prepared and made available to all boards.

In September 1987, the Report of the Provincial Advisory Committee on Race Relations was released by the ministry for validation. A series of six regional conferences was held at which trustees, administrators, other related school personnel (as well as representatives of community groups) viewed a video on Race and

Ethnocultural Equity commissioned by the ministry to introduce the report and highlight the importance of policy development in this area. Workshops were held at these conferences on each area of the report and the validation process explained.

Over a 6-month period, written reactions to the report were received and summarized by the ministry in a document entitled "A Synopsis of Public Responses to the Report of the Provincial Advisory Committee on Race Relations: *The Development of a Policy on Race and Ethnocultural Equity*", September 1988.

There were several issues concerning both policy development and implementation raised by the respondents in the validation procedure. In general, there was support given to the importance of community involvement and input from racial and ethnocultural minority groups. Many emphasized that an overall policy on race and ethnocultural equity should be mandated by the Ministry of Education. It was also generally agreed that boards should ensure that they effectively market their equity policies when developed.

The two most repeated themes in the validation responses were funding and leadership. The synopsis states that "a majority of respondents focused on the need for financial support from the Ministry (to support both policy development and implementation) as well as the need for Ministry direction and leadership in all aspects of the development, implementation, and monitoring of this policy". It was recognized that boards that have already developed and begun implementing a policy could be very useful resources to boards who have yet to do so and respondents generally look to the ministry to provide both leadership and support in assisting boards to obtain the resources they need to develop and implement policies effectively in their own jurisdictions.

It is the latter issue that provides the rationale for the present study. In order to develop a comprehensive strategy to assist school boards across the province to develop and implement policies on race and ethnocultural equity, it is important to determine the number of boards that actually have policies, what stage others are at, what similarities and differences exist in the policies themselves, what the perceived needs are of boards at various stages of policy development and implementation, and how these might vary in different regions across the province.

In order to provide useful resources and guidelines for school boards in the area of race and ethnocultural equity policy development and implementation, the present study was designed to gather existing policy documents, to identify the barriers to and key factors in success of policy development and implementation, and to make recommendations to the ministry to facilitate the process for school boards across Ontario. Specifically, the purpose of the present study was as follows:

1. To collect and compile the available documentation on school board race and ethnocultural policy development and implementation directives, such that it can be used as a resource for other boards.

2. To analyze the content of the existing policies and the processes of development and implementation to determine if particular variables lead to particular models and outcomes.

3. To review both the needs expressed by school board personnel and the literature on race and ethnocultural issues in school situations, with emphasis on Canadian material.

4. To make specific recommendations for action and research, based on the literature, the actual policies and procedures, and the findings from survey and interview data.

METHOD

A survey and interview approach were used for this investigation. The constraints of time (four months in total) played a major part in dictating that efficiency be a prime consideration in methodology. An effort was made to achieve the best possible response rate from school boards in the short time available by following up the questionnaires with a second mailing. Interviews were conducted in person and by telephone to give detailed insight into the questionnaire results.

<u>Phase 1</u> (February 1989) consisted of the collection of policies, supporting documentation, and curriculum resources in race and ethnocultural equity. These were gathered through Survey I, which consisted of a letter to the 21 boards that were known by the researchers and contacts to have policies (see Appendix B1). This material was collected and compiled in large binders, which are at present in the office of the Deputy Minister of Education. Inquiries are being made into the most efficient way of making this information available to school boards. The binders also include summary sheets with an analysis of the content of the policies. Consultation was also held at this stage with the Regional Race Relations Officers of the Ministry of Education; regular progress reports have been submitted to them.

<u>Phase 2</u> (March/April 1989) included a review of the available literature on aspects of race and ethnocultural equity such as curriculum, assessment, racial incidents, and others. A selected resource bibliography is included in this report, with an emphasis on **Canadian research and material**. The second part of Phase 2 was the sending of a letter and questionnaire to all 124 school boards listed in the Canadian Education Association's directory asking them to send race and ethnocultural equity policies, supporting documents, and related policies, and to complete the questionnaire (see Appendixes B2 and B3). All correspondence in this study was sent to the director who then either completed the questionnaire him/herself or asked the person in the board most familiar with these issues to do it (e.g. race relations consultant, multiculturalism co-ordinator, or a superintendent or staff person chairing the committee).

The combined response to Surveys I and II was excellent. In some cases, boards sent policies, and in other cases they sent questionnaire responses. A follow-up questionnaire was sent to cut down the number of non-respondents and a total of 100 responses (out of a possible 124) eventually received (Appendix B5). Usable questionnaires totalled 84 (31 boards with policies and 53 boards without policies), since some of the boards that sent policies in Survey I did not complete the follow-up questionnaire. These were included in the interview sample to ensure follow-up.

Phase 3 (April/May 1989) consisted of in-depth interviews with key personnel of selected boards that had developed policies. The purpose of the interviews was to explore the actual process of policy development and implementation and to learn about local factors that might shape the process. A standardized interview protocol was drawn up and interviews were conducted in person or by telephone in the various regions (Appendix B4). In addition to interviewing several boards in Metropolitan Toronto, visits were made to London, Windsor, Hamilton, Waterloo, Ottawa, Parry Sound, and Timmins. In all, 43 interviews were conducted with people from 22 school boards. The names of school boards interviewed are not listed in this report to protect confidentiality. The interviews gave insights into how the policy was developed and why certain boards had policies that did not seem to be in the process of effective implementation, as well as what the political processes were behind the development and implementation of the policy.

Particular attention was paid in interviews to eliciting the relationship of race and ethnocultural equity policy to francophone and aboriginal communities, and to the concerns of Northern and Southern Ontario. Finally, school boards were sent letters of thanks and were informed that plans were being investigated about ways to make available to them the resources them on policy development that were gathered in the course of this project (Appendix B6).

RESULTS

POLICIES AND DOCUMENTS ON RACE AND ETHNOCULTURAL EQUITY

The first survey letter (See Appendix B) was sent out to the 21 school boards that the researchers and local contact people knew had policies on race and ethnocultural equity. The boards supplied copies of their policy statements and supporting documents. The original 21 boards contacted are shown in Appendix A1.

Titles and Terminology

Only policies developed very recently, following the ministry's draft report, have the concept of equity in the title, usually race and ethnocultural equity.

Boards that developed policies in the 1970s and early 1980s used the terms multiculturalism and/or race relations in the titles, often for separate documents. This terminology gave way to a more holistic approach in the mid-1980s, including the use of several terms in the titles of policies, e.g., multicultural, ethnic and/or race relations policy or race and ethnocultural policy. The documents themselves and later follow-up interviews revealed that most school board personnel clearly prefer positive, pro-active language in the policy document and in most boards there is a reluctance to use the term anti-racist education, especially in the title.

The lengthier policy documents have glossaries appended. Definitions of terms vary, signalling the importance of clarifying the language used.

Format and Structure of Policies

Although the structure and format of the policy documents differ significantly from board to board, they appear to be of four types:

1. Full reports of committees, containing background, rationale, and a lengthy list of recommendations - average length 40 pages.

2. Policy Statements, with preambles in prose form and/or explanatory sections following the statements - average length 10 pages.

3. Policy Statements with preambles, explanation, and specific administrative procedures attached to each statement - average length 25 pages.

4. Policy Statements with few or no explanatory notes and no implementation procedures - average length 2 pages.

Those in the first two categories often have some historical development included, as well as a glossary of terms and a bibliography of resources. Boards use other boards' documents as models for their own, but structure them in a way that suits the "culture" of their board. Some were careful to have the format of the policy match all other internal board documents. Others packaged the policy very distinctively in an attempt to "market" the concepts effectively.

The interviews revealed that boards that chose to have the policy look like all other policies did so for one of two reasons. Some boards felt it should look exactly like other policies so it could be given as much importance and be seen to fit into the overall philosophy and structure of the board, to the point of being included in the corporate plan. Others believed that the policy (and process) should not be distinctive and, in fact, be played down somewhat so that people would not have the idea that it was different from any other policy and be threatened by that.

It is important to note further that the interviews revealed that policies of the latter type have less likelihood of being implemented. Boards that recognize that policies to achieve race and ethnocultural equity are different from other policies (because their content is so value-oriented and emotionally laden and because they affect the entire system - staff, students and community) are far more likely to develop a policy and a process to maximize the likelihood of effective implementation.

Content Areas

The chart on the following three pages presents a summary of the areas covered in the policy documents received by April 30, 1989. It may be noted that the content areas of most policies include:
Assessment and Placement of Students
Curriculum Development and Implementation
School/Community Relations
Employment Practices
Staff Development
Dealing with Incidents of Expressed Bias and Discrimination (also called Handling Racial and Ethnic Incidents)

TABLE 1
OVERVIEW OF SCHOOL BOARD POLICIES

PUBLIC SCHOOL BOARDS	DOCUMENT TITLE & DATE	SCHOOL COMMUNITY RELATIONS	CURRICULUM DEVELOPMENT	EMPLOYMENT STAFF DEVELOPMENT	DEALING WITH INCIDENTS OF BIAS AND DISCRIMINATION	ASSESSMENT PLACEMENT OF STUDENT	OTHER MATERIAL SUBMITTED
1. Cochrane-Iroquois Falls, Black River - Matheson	Multicultural Ethnic and Race Relations Draft/April '89						
2. Durham	The Development of Race & Ethno-cultural Equity Policy, April '89	Yes	Yes	Yes	Yes Race & Ethno-cultural Harassment	Yes	Leadership Research
3. East York	Multicultural Ethnic and Race Relations April '87	Yes	Yes	Yes	Yes	Yes	Resource, Dev. of Policy Background & Stages Glossary
4. Elgin							
5. Etobicoke	Race and Ethnic Relations Policy Implementation & Review Process '87	Yes	Yes	Yes	Yes	Reception Assessment Placement	Co-curricular Prog. Admin. Regulations Visitors

10

PUBLIC SCHOOL BOARDS	DOCUMENT TITLE & DATE	SCHOOL COMMUNITY RELATIONS	CURRICULUM DEVELOPMENT	EMPLOYMENT STAFF DEVELOPMENT	DEALING WITH INCIDENTS OF BIAS AND DISCRIMINATION	ASSESSMENT PLACEMENT OF STUDENT	OTHER MATERIAL SUBMITTED
6. Frontenac	The Response of the Frontenac County Board of Education to the Report of the Provincial Advisory Committee on Race Relations Feb '88	Community-Based Discussions	Yes	Report on the Activities of the Employment Equity Program 1987/88			Report of the Sub-committee to examine barriers to employment
7. Hamilton	Towards a Race Relations and Ethnocultural Equity Policy '89	Yes	Yes	Employment Practices	Responding to Harassment	Special Services	Leadership Initiatives Resources
8. Huron County	Policy Statements on Multicultural and Race Relations Sept. '88	Yes	Yes	Yes			
9. Kirkland Lake	Race and Ethno-cultural Relations Feb '88		Yes	Employment Equity			
10. Lambton	Human Relations Policy and Regulations '87	Committee	Yes	Yes		Student needs Student Welcoming	Resource, Policy and Curriculum

11

PUBLIC SCHOOL BOARDS	DOCUMENT TITLE & DATE	SCHOOL COMMUNITY RELATIONS	CURRICULUM DEVELOPMENT	EMPLOYMENT STAFF DEVELOPMENT	DEALING WITH INCIDENTS OF BIAS AND DISCRIMINATION	ASSESSMENT PLACEMENT OF STUDENT	OTHER MATERIAL SUBMITTED
11. London	Multicultural Race & Ethnic Relations June '88	Yes	Yes	Yes	Yes	Assessment Counselling & Placement	Glossary & Bibliography Student Programs Policy Development
12. Nipigon-Red Rock							Racial Harassment
13. North York	Race and Ethnic Relations Pol. & Proced. '81	Yes	Yes	Yes	Yes	Yes	School Visitors Bibliography
14. Ottawa	Race & Ethnic Relations - A Policy Stmnt '84	Yes	Yes	Yes	Yes	Yes	Special Programs ESL, Heritage, Awareness
15. Peel	Multiculturalism Race Relations Feb '88	Yes	Yes	Yes	Harassment Pol. being developed	Yes	Equal Opportunity
16. Scarborough	Race Relations, Ethnic Relations & Multicultural Policy '87	Yes	Yes	Yes	Racial and Ethnocultural Harassment	Yes	Leadership, ESL, ESD, Translated Materials Resources
17. Stormont, Dundas & Glengarry County							

PUBLIC SCHOOL BOARDS	DOCUMENT TITLE & DATE	SCHOOL COMMUNITY RELATIONS	CURRICULUM DEVELOPMENT	EMPLOYMENT STAFF DEVELOPMENT	DEALING WITH INCIDENTS OF BIAS AND DISCRIMINATION	ASSESSMENT PLACEMENT OF STUDENT	OTHER MATERIAL SUBMITTED
18. Timiskaming	Race & Ethnocultural Relations in the Education System '87	Yes	Yes	Yes	Race & Ethnocultural Practices Admin. Regulations	Yes	Co-Curricular Act. Heritage Lang.
19. Timmins	Race & Ethnocultural Relations Policy Stmnt '88	Yes	Yes	Yes	Race & Ethnocultural Practices Admin. Regulations	Yes	Co-Curricular Act. Heritage Lang.
20. Toronto	Final Report of Sub-committee on Race Relations May '79		Yes	Yes	Yes	Yes	Extra Curric. Act. In Service Resources
21. Victoria	Multicultural Race Relations April '87		Yes	Yes	Yes		Statement of Philosophy Glossary
22. Waterloo	Race and Ethnocultural Relations Pol. & Proced. Feb. '88		Yes	Yes	Racial & Ethnocultural Harassment		Leadership, Background, Glossary
23. West Parry Sound	Race and Ethnocultural Equity A Policy Oct. '88	Yes	Yes	Affirmative Action Employment Equity Policy Guidelines			Co-Curricular Act. Ont. Policy on Race Relations

PUBLIC SCHOOL BOARDS	DOCUMENT TITLE & DATE	SCHOOL COMMUNITY RELATIONS	CURRICULUM DEVELOPMENT	EMPLOYMENT STAFF DEVELOPMENT	DEALING WITH INCIDENTS OF BIAS AND DISCRIMINATION	ASSESSMENT PLACEMENT OF STUDENT	OTHER MATERIAL SUBMITTED
24. Windsor	Race Relations Policy - Mar. '85		Yes	System & Staff Development	Responses to Racial Incidents		Co-ordinator School Activities Resources
25. York	Report of the Race Relations Committee '79			In-service Training	Procedure & Follow-up		Initiatives to Promote Awareness Resources
26. York Region	An Approach to Multiculturalism In Area E Schools Nov '86		Yes			Reception, Assessment Placement of ESL Students	Establishing an Advisory Committee on Race Relations needs Assmnt. Surv.

SEPARATE SCHOOL BOARDS	DOCUMENT TITLE & DATE	SCHOOL COMMUNITY RELATIONS	CURRICULUM DEVELOPMENT	EMPLOYMENT STAFF DEVELOPMENT	DEALING WITH INCIDENTS OF BIAS AND DISCRIMINATION	ASSESSMENT PLACEMENT OF STUDENT	OTHER MATERIAL SUBMITTED
1. Brant	Policy on Multi-culturalism April '88	Yes	Yes		Yes	Yes	ESL, Heritage Language
2. Bruce-Grey	Policy on Workplace Harassment '88				Racial or Ethnic Harassment		Religious Studies Family Life Studies Units
3. Carleton	Policy on Race & Ethnic Relations	Yes	Yes	Yes	Yes	Yes	Leadership
4. Dufferin-Peel	Multiculturalism and Race Relations Policy – Drft '88	Yes	Yes	Yes	Yes	Student Services	Con. Ed., Glossary Resources
5. Durham	Race Relations and Ethnocultural Equity – Oct. '88	Yes	Yes	Yes	Yes	Yes	Leadership, Research Support Service In Guidance
6. Essex	Race and Ethnic Relations – Feb '89	Yes	Yes	Yes	Yes	Yes	Leadership, Research Aim & Objectives, Glossary, Bibliog.
7. Frontenac-Lennox & Addington	Race Relations & Ethnocultural Equity, Drft '88	Yes	Yes	Yes	Racial Harmony Admin. Regulation	Student Support Services	
8. Huron-Perth	Race, Ethnic & Multicultural Relations Jan. '89	Yes	Yes	Yes	Yes		
9. Lakehead District				Employment Equity			Mission Statement

SEPARATE SCHOOL BOARDS	DOCUMENT TITLE & DATE	SCHOOL COMMUNITY RELATIONS	CURRICULUM DEVELOPMENT	EMPLOYMENT STAFF DEVELOPMENT	DEALING WITH INCIDENTS OF BIAS AND DISCRIMINATION	ASSESSMENT PLACEMENT OF STUDENT	OTHER MATERIAL SUBMITTED
10. London & Middlesex County	Race & Ethno-cultural Relations Policy, Drft '89		Regulations and Procedures will be established through the office of the Director of Education				Statement of Aims & Objectives
11. Metro	Race & Ethnic Relations and Multicultural Policy '84	Yes	Yes	Yes	Yes	Special Services	Leadership Init. Glossary Resources
12. Timiskaming District	Race and Ethno-cultural Relations in the Education System - Oct '87	Yes	Yes	Yes	Race & Ethno-cultural Practices	Yes	Heritage Language
13. Timmins District							
14. Waterloo Region	Meeting the Challenge - Race Religious & Ethno-cultural equity Drft '89	Yes	Yes	Yes	Yes	Yes	Leadership Init. Communications Bibliog. Glossary
15. Windsor							
16. York Region	Multiculturalism and Race Relations Pol. & Proced Oct. '85	Yes	Yes	Yes	Yes	Yes	Policy Statement ESL Programs

Since most boards use other boards' policies as resource documents, it is not surprising that there is a great deal of overlap in the content areas covered. These areas are consistent with those used in the document "Towards a Policy", introduced at the joint conference in March 1986. The greatest number of support documents submitted was in the area of curriculum (including co-curricular programs), leadership camps, heritage languages, Native Studies and Black Studies. A few boards have developed guidelines for handling racial incidents, as this tends to be one of the first procedural documents developed after a policy is passed. Some also had supporting pamphlets and regular newsletters describing the policy and providing updated information and resources as they became available.

If there is an area that is likely to be omitted in a policy, it is school/community relations. Staffing (employment practices) and staff development are frequently combined in the same area or staff development may be included as a component of all the other areas, and so may not have a specific section devoted to it. The one- or two-page policy documents are usually not divided into content areas, but tend to have an overall policy statement followed by some specific statements, usually dealing with handling racial incidents or harassment.

QUESTIONNAIRE ON RACIAL AND ETHNOCULTURAL EQUITY

In the second phase of the research, a letter and questionnaire were sent to the 124 school boards in the province listed in the CEA directory including 10 francophone sections of boards. The findings from this survey are divided into two components: a) data on school policies and b) questionnaire responses on policy development.

a) <u>Data on School Board Policies</u>

The 97 responses to Survey II yielded, in total, confirmation of 39 policies and 3 draft policies on racial and ethnocultural equity in existence throughout the province. These policies, including the ones submitted in Survey II are listed by region in Table 2.

It can be clearly seen from Table 2 that such policies have been developed primarily in the urban southern areas of the province, but by no means exclusively.

Survey II also asked school boards to state clearly whether they did **not** have an overall policy, and the results of this inquiry are shown by region in Tables 3 and 4. The names of boards which are **in the process** of developing an overall policy are shown in Table 3. The names of 37 boards claiming not to have an overall policy are shown in Table 4.

TABLE 2

BOARDS WITH POLICIES BY REGION

	Public	Separate
Central Region	1. Durham 2. East York 3. Etobicoke 4. Hamilton 5. North York 6. Peel 7. Scarborough 8. Toronto 9. Victoria County 10. Waterloo County 11. York City	12. Brant 13. Dufferin Peel 14. Durham 15. Metropolitan Toronto 16. Waterloo Region* 17. York Region
Eastern Region	18. Frontenac * 19. Ottawa 20. Stormont, Dundas, & Glengarry	21. Carleton 22. Frontenac, Lennox & Addington
Midnorthern		
Northeastern	23. Cochrane-Iroquois Falls* 24. Hearst 25. Kirkland Lake 26. Timiskaming 27. Timmins 28. West Parry Sound	29. Timiskaming District 30. Timmins District
Northwestern	31. Nipigon-Red Rock	32. Lakehead District **
Western	33. Elgin County* 34. Huron County 35. Lambton County 36. London 37. Windsor	38. Essex County 39. Huron-Perth 40. London & Middlesex County 41. Windsor 42 Bruce-Grey County

* At draft stage

** Administrative policy only

TABLE 3

BOARDS DEVELOPING A POLICY BY REGION

	<u>Public</u>	<u>Separate</u>
Central Region	1. Halton 2. Niagara South 3. Wellington County 4. York Region	5. Halton 6. Hamilton-Wentworth 7. Simcoe County 8. Welland County
Eastern	9. Carleton 10. Leeds and Grenville	11. Ottawa
Midnorthern	12. Manitoulin 13. Sudbury	
Northwestern	14. Kenora 15. Lake Superior 16. Lakehead	
Western	17. Essex County 18. Kent County 19. Middlesex County 20. Oxford County 21. Perth County	22. Kent County

NOTE: York Region is included in <u>Tables 3 and 4</u> since it is developing a new policy.

TABLE 4

BOARDS WITH NO OVERALL POLICY BY REGION

	Public	Separate
Central Region	1. Brant County 2. Haldimand 3. Haliburton County 4. Hastings County 5. Norfolk 6. Northumberland and Newcastle 7. Peterborough County 8. Prince Edward County 9. Simcoe County 10. York Region	11. Haldimand-Norfolk 12. Hastings-Prince Edward County 13. Lincoln County 14. Peterborough, Victoria, Northumberland & Newcastle
Eastern	15. Lennox & Addington 16. Ottawa-Carleton (French)	17. Lanark, Leeds & Grenville County
Midnorthern	18. Central Algoma 19. Espanola 20. Michipicoten 21. North Shore 22. Sault Ste. Marie	23. North Shore District 24. Sault Ste. Marie District
Northeastern	25. East Parry Sound 26. Nipissing	27. Cochrane Iroquois Falls-Black River Matheson (French) 28. Kapuskasing (French) 29. Nipissing District
Northwestern	30. Fort Francis-Rainy River 31. Geraldton 32. Red Lake	33. Dryden District 34. Geraldton District 35. North of Superior
Western	36. Bruce County	37. Lambton County

NOTE: York Region is included in Tables 3 and 4 since it is developing a new policy.

The school boards were also asked if they had policies and procedures that, while not specifically titled as such, related closely to racial and ethnocultural equity issues. The areas that were specified were assessment and placement, school-community relations, employment practices, handling racial incidents, and assessment curriculm adapted from those found in the Report of the Provincial Advisory Committee *The Development of a Policy on Race and Ethnocultural Equity*, with the addition of heritage language and native studies.

The answers to this question show a clear pattern. Boards that have an overall policy are also far more likely to have produced policies and supporting documents in closely linked areas. The figures are shown in Table 5. A clear comparison can be seen by examining the bar graph in Figure 1. The greatest frequency of related policy and support documents is in the area of personnel policies and practices, with boards specifically mentioning race and ethnocultural equity issues in their personnel policies, rather than only gender issues.

The greatest discrepancy between boards with and without overall policies was in the area of support documents for curriculum (bar A).

The greatest similarity was in support documents for native studies (bar F). However, overall, Figure 1 shows a consistently higher proportion of support documents in boards with overall policies.

It is not merely having a policy that results in additional materials, but there does appear to be several factors responsible for this finding. Many of the boards with policies are large urban boards that have more resources for developing specialized policies as well as further support documents. Many are boards that have a long history of involvement in multicultural education and heritage language teaching, and the documents in these areas are linked with concern for race and ethnocultural equity.

The development of separate policies concerning incidents of racial harassment (bar E) is also significantly low in boards with no overall policy. It might be deduced that employment issues are easier to deal with (particularly with the province's pay equity legislation in place) than the issue of racial harassment. Of course the Ministry of Education's incentive funding for the development of affirmative action or equal employment opportunity policies for women clearly had an impact in this area.

TABLE 5

BOARDS WITH AND WITHOUT POLICIES WHICH HAVE DOCUMENTS IN OTHER AREAS

	N		A	B	C	D	E	F	G	H	I	J	N/R
Boards with Policies	31	(N)	16	17	13	15	14	7	25	16	11	3	3
		(%)	52	55	42	48	45	23	81	52	35	10	10
Boards without Policies	53	(N)	1	15	10	3	3	15	31	17	12	4	13
		(%)	2	28	19	6	6	28	58	32	23	8	25

A - Multi-racial and anti-racist curriculum
B - Heritage Language
C - School and community relations
D - Testing and assessment of non-English or non-French speakers
E - Documentation of incidents of racial harassment
F - Native studies
G - Personnel policies and practices, e.g., employment equity
H - Staff development
I - Support services in guidance
J - Other
N/R - No response

FIGURE 1

PERCENTAGES OF BOARDS WITH AND WITHOUT POLICIES WITH DOCUMENTATION IN OTHER AREAS

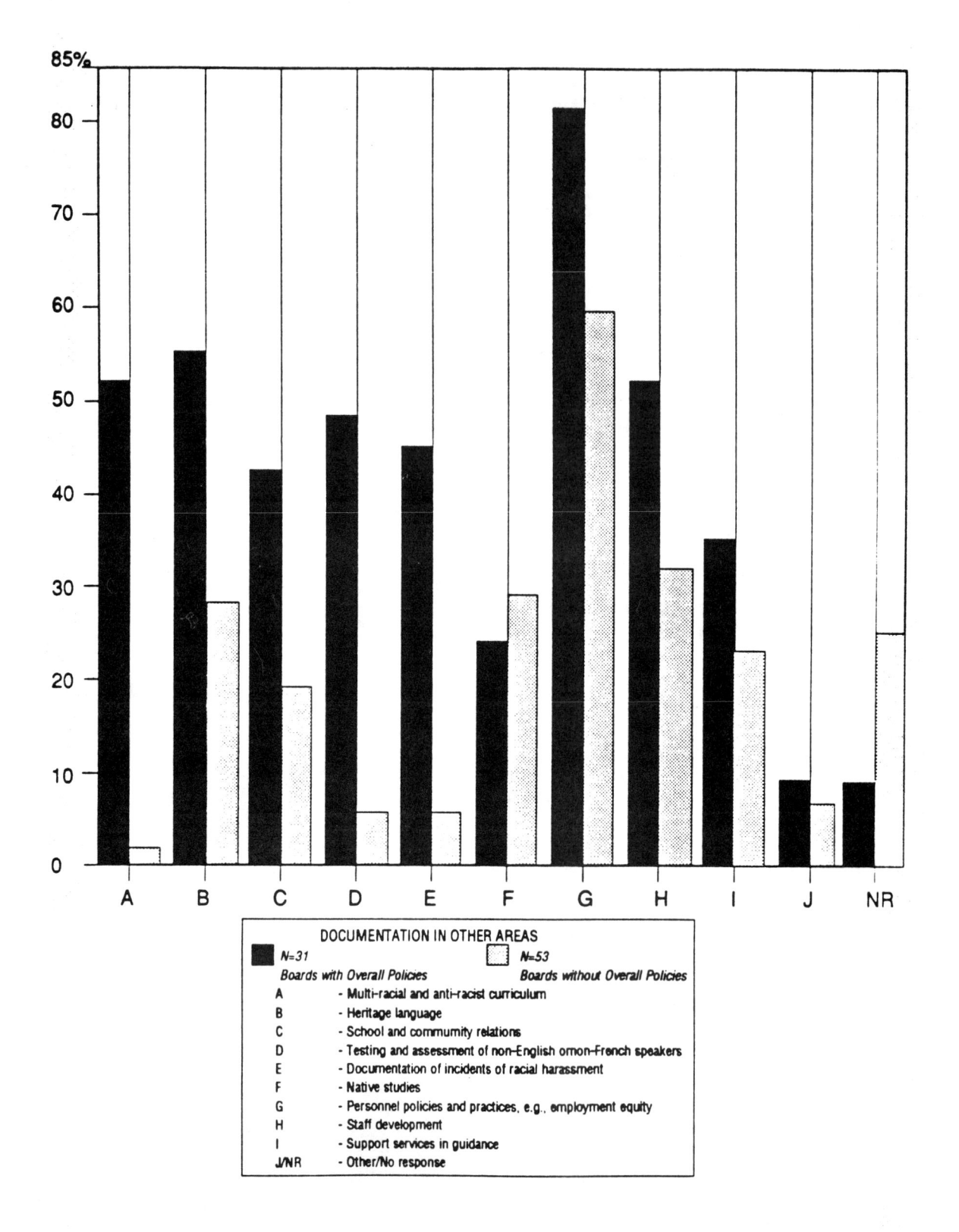

DOCUMENTATION IN OTHER AREAS

■ N=31   ▢ N=53
Boards with Overall Policies   Boards without Overall Policies

- A - Multi-racial and anti-racist curriculum
- B - Heritage language
- C - School and community relations
- D - Testing and assessment of non-English ornon-French speakers
- E - Documentation of incidents of racial harassment
- F - Native studies
- G - Personnel policies and practices, e.g., employment equity
- H - Staff development
- I - Support services in guidance
- J/NR - Other/No response

It was beyond the scope of this survey to inquire as to why boards have not developed an overall policy. However, the responses to this question show that the process of developing related documents is in some way tied in with the overall policy development process. If boards do not have a policy, it is less likely they will have other materials in this area. Boards that do not have policies are more likely to be disproportionately in rural areas or in Northern Ontario. They are also likely to be smaller boards with fewer resources. As will be shown in the interview data, the two other intervening variables are the political or administrative will to develop a policy and/or a catalytic incident that compels boards to begin the process. Several small, rural and northern boards have put considerable effort into policy development because the will existed to take action and the time was right.

Data on the Process of Policy Development

All of the above results relate to the actual documents themselves. The remainder of the data dealt with the process of policy development. To determine the role of the Ministry of Education in the process, we asked boards if they had participated in the process of validation of the ministry document *The Development of a Policy on Race and Ethnocultural Equity*. The responses are shown in Table 6.

These responses do not show a clear pattern that the validation process acted as a catalyst to the policy development process. However, it is more likely that boards not participating in the process also do not now have a policy. On the other hand, the interview data reveal that school personnel interpreted this question to refer only to the formal process of submitting written briefs to the Ministry of Education. In fact, many of them remembered having attended one of the six regional meetings and refer to their attendance at that meeting as an impetus to developing the policy.

Likewise, not everyone responded to the next question, on the follow-up to participation in the validation process. However, the results are shown in Table 7 because they reveal the qualitative responses to the question. Generally speaking, the boards that followed up on the validation process appear to be ones that already had existing structures that could be adapted for policy development in this area.

One of the most interesting findings of the research was found in responses to the next question, which asked the respondent to state how far along they perceived

TABLE 6

PARTICIPATION IN VALIDATION OF MINISTRY DOCUMENT
BY BOARDS WITH A POLICY AND BOARDS WITHOUT A POLICY

	Participated	Did Not Participate	Not Sure	N/R	Total
Boards with a Policy	18	11	1	1	31
Boards without a Policy	16	37	-	-	53
	34	48	1	1	84

TABLE 7

FOLLOW-UP TO THE VALIDATION PROCESS
IN ORDER OF FREQUENCY

BOARDS WITH POLICY

Committee and Policy Development (6)

Group that Participation Provided Feedback Re: Validation Process (3)

Provided Input to Various Committees Developing Race Relations Papers (2)

Increased Awareness (1)

Attended Training Sessions by the Ministry of Citizenship (1)

Undertaking the Implementation of the Policy (1)

Draft was used as the Basis for an Action Plan (1)

Reports forwarded to the Ministry of Education (1)

BOARDS WITHOUT POLICY

Established a Committee for Policy Development (4)

Started Internal Discussions (2)

In Process of Preparing Working our Own Policy and Procedures (2)

Policy Development Between 1989-92 (1)

Sent Staff to Conferences on Awareness (1)

Waiting Public Response (1)

themselves to be in the policy development process. The purpose of this question was to ensure that boards that had already done work on their policies would have this fact acknowledged in this report.

The responses to the question, however, reveal an unanticipated finding. The subjective perception of a board's progress is not always in accord with the other "hard" evidence that boards send. In other words, as can be seen clearly in Figure 2, there are differences in the perception of boards' progress in policy development. Some boards state they have "no policy" and yet are well along the path of policy development to the point of an extensive draft in the validation process. Other boards state that they do have a policy, and yet it may encompass only a very small part of the total picture. As can be seen in Figure 2, boards at early, middle, and late stages of policy development sometimes claim to have a policy and sometimes do not. Thus the fact that 54 boards claim to have no policy should not obscure the far more optimistic picture that 25 of these boards are actively working on a policy. The numerical breakdown is shown in Table 8. The high number of "Other" among school boards without an overall policy is partially explained by some 10 boards who noted that aspects of race and ethnocultural equity policy are embedded in other policy areas in their board. The other 13 responses are qualitative and the comments are summarized as follows:

1. Need guidelines from the ministry.
2. Need money and personnel.
3. All are treated equally, therefore there is no need for policy.
4. Waiting for the results of the task force re: school for the retarded.
5. Philosophy clearly states that each child will be treated in a Christian fashion.
6. Doing an assessment of the board's needs.
7. Nothing has been done.
8. Awaiting ministry resource book.
9. Racial and ethnocultural policies embedded in policies in our board.
10. We are in the early stages.

FIGURE 2

PERCEPTIONS OF LEVEL OF POLICY DEVELOPMENT BY BOARDS WITH AND WITHOUT OVERALL POLICIES

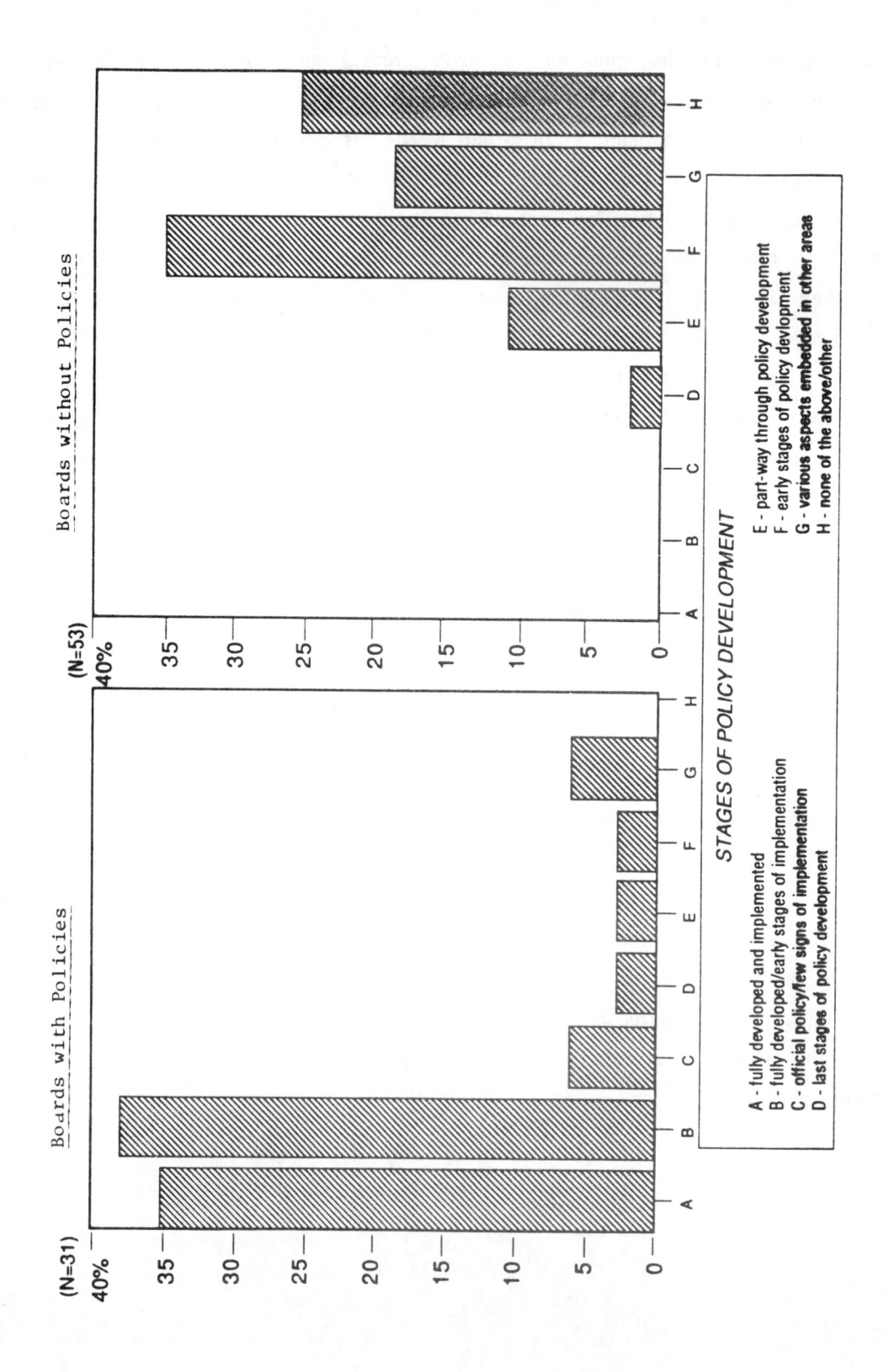

STAGES OF POLICY DEVELOPMENT

A - fully developed and implemented
B - fully developed/early stages of implementation
C - official policy/few signs of implementation
D - last stages of policy development
E - part-way through policy development
F - early stages of policy development
G - various aspects embedded in other areas
H - none of the above/other

TABLE 8

STAGE OF POLICY DEVELOPMENT BY BOARDS
WITH AND WITHOUT POLICY

	Fully Developed or Official	Last Stages	Part Way	Early Stages	Other	N/R	Total
Boards with Policy	25	1	1	1	2	1	31
Boards without Policy	0	1	6	19	23	4	53
	25	2	7	20	25	5	84

TABLE 9

THE MAIN RACIAL AND ETHNOCULTURAL MINORITY GROUPS
(IN ORDER OF MAGNITUDE)

BOARDS WITH OVERALL POLICY		BOARDS WITHOUT OVERALL POLICY	
ITALIAN	14	NATIVE	18
NATIVE	7	PORTUGUESE	12
PORTUGUESE	7	ASIAN	12
ASIAN	7	ITALIAN	11
EUROPEAN	5	GERMANIC	8
GREEK	4	EAST INDIAN	6
BLACK	2	FRENCH	
CHINESE	2	UKRAINIAN	
EAST ASIAN		FINNISH	
ORIENTAL		POLISH	
EAST INDIAN			
JEWISH			
ARABIC			
SPANISH/GERMAN			
INDO-ASIAN			
WEST INDIAN			
LEBANESE			
GERMAN			

The questions of why some boards are of the opinion that there is no need to develop a policy is beyond the scope of the current study. However, the responses indicate that resources are scarce for this task; it is considered that other policies or philosophies encompass this area; or people do not see the need because they are experiencing no problems in their area.

To give some insight into the clientele served by schools with or without a policy, boards were asked to estimate the relative size of racial or ethnocultural minority groups within their jurisdiction. For the francophone sample, the word "linguistic" was also added. The results were as shown on Table 9.

For the four largest minority groups, the results are shown in condensed form in Table 10. It appears that boards without policies are more likely to have native children in their jurisdictions than those with policies. Since many boards are in the urban south, this fact would be partially explained by geography. But the eighteen boards without policies that are serving native children are all rural southern or northern boards. Once again, there are several variables responsible for this finding. The resources available and size of board may be key factors in hindering policy development, while the actual ethnic composition of the clientele may be of secondary importance. However, the interview data from Northern Ontario indicate that aboriginal people feel in some cases that their needs are being ignored. The term "ethnocultural" is being interpreted to refer to immigrant groups rather than to first nations peoples.

The fact that the process of policy development is subject to a wide variety of interpretation is a point that has already been made, but it becomes even more evident in the responses to the rest of the questionnaire. Boards were asked what processes and personnel were involved in policy development. The responses are listed in Table 11.

TABLE 10

FOUR MAIN MINORITY GROUPS BY
BOARDS WITH OR WITHOUT POLICY

	NATIVE	ITALIAN	PORTUGUESE	ASIAN
BOARDS WITH POLICY	7	14	7	7
BOARDS WITHOUT POLICY	18	11	12	12

TABLE 11

THE PROCESS AND PERSONNEL INVOLVED IN POLICY
DEVELOPMENT AND IMPLEMENTATION

	BOARDS WITH POLICIES		BOARDS WITHOUT POLICIES
PROCESS: 8	Investigative Committees	7	Steering Committee
6	Board Approval	2	Research
3	System and Community Groups for Evaluation	2	Preparing Options
3	Requested Submissions from Interest Groups/Individuals	2	Copies of Other Policies
2	Policy Originated from Heritage Language Policy	1	Committees & Budget Established
2	Vetted by Parent/Teacher and Community Groups	1	Development of Procedure for Hiring
2	Committee of Representatives With the System Drafted from Ministry Document	1	Tuition Agreement with Indian Band
2	Questionnaires	1	Invitations to All Organizations Within the Board
2	Meetings, Workshops	1	Draft Copy Derived from Other Boards
1	Draft to Board for Readings	1	Working Committee
1	Policy Under Systems Review	1	Process/Timelines
1	Co-operatively Developed with Neighbouring Boards	1	Interest Groups Submit Policy Issues
1	Board Committee Identified Need	1	System and Interest Groups for Evaluation
1	Policy Drafted from Resource Ministry of Education		

TABLE 11 (Cont'd)

1	Participated in the Process of Validation		
1	Drafted by Principal		
1	Vetted by Executive Council		
1	Feedback From Multi-cultural Advisory Committee		
PERSONNEL:16	Teaching and Non-Teaching Staff Administration	10	Senior Academic Officials
13	Trustees, Board Members	9	Staff
13	Community Leaders/ Groups Unions	7	Community Groups
5	Race Relations	2	Human Resources Department
1	Representatives from Board Departments and Employee Groups	2	Religious Dept.
1	Federation Representatives	1	Native Trustees Native Agencies
1	Parent-Teacher Associations and Parishes		

ALTERNATIVES TO POLICY DEVELOPMENT:

2	Integrated Studies
1	Heritage Language
1	Special Events/Days

TABLE 12

FACTORS WHICH LED TO SUCCESS IN THE DEVELOPMENT OF POLICY

		BOARDS WITH POLICIES		BOARDS WITHOUT POLICIES
MINISTRY RELATED:	1	Ministry Initiatives	2	Encouragement From Ministry
	1	Employment Equity Initiatives		
	1	Input from Ministry		
BOARD RELATED:	6	Committment of Trustees	1	Board Committment
	5	Support from Senior Administration and Trustees		
	1	Involvement of Diverse Groups of Board Members		
	1	Recognition from Board of Importance		
	1	Appointment of Consultant		
	1	Board's Multicultural Advisory Committee		
SCHOOL RELATED:	4	Staff Commitment	1	Administration Committed to Results
	1	Strong Leadership from Senior Administration	1	Involvement from all Staff
	2	Input from Teachers Federation	1	Acceptance through In-Service
	1	Concentrated Effort By Staff		
COMMUNITY RELATED:	4	Community Input		
	4	Community Concern		
	2	Interest Within the Community		
	1	Initiative of Human Rights Officer		

TABLE 12 (Cont'd)

OTHER:	3	Small Focused Group With Training and Time Allotted	2	Appreciation of Others
	2	To Prevent Race Relation Problems	2	Relates to the Board's Catholic Philosophy of Education
	1	Implentation Program		
	1	Relatedness of Topic		
	1	Commitment of Affirmative Action Committee		
	1	Catholic Mandate		
	1	Skilled Writing Team		
	1	Willingness to Serve All with Equality		
	1	Political Will (1977)		
	1	Climate for Development		

The comparison of the two lists shows that boards that have developed policies have access to a wider network of personnel and resources and tend to look beyond their own local leaders. Boards without policies note fewer resources for the process itself and tend to draw on a more localized circle of personnel. These findings are consistent with the findings that boards with policies are more likely to be in urban Southern Ontario where there are more accessible resources in this area.

Factors that led (or are leading) to success in the development of policy are noted in Table 12. The first evident finding is that boards without policies have noted fewer factors, mostly because they are not as far advanced in the process. The responses from boards with policies also tend to be more specific and more wide-ranging. It is noteworthy that no boards without policies cited community involvement as a factor in success.

Factors that were cited as preventing success are listed in Table 13. However, on comparison, it is apparent that the lists are based on different assumptions. The factors cited by boards with policies tend to be ones that they have overcome, whereas the factors cited by boards without policies are those that are actually preventing the development of policy at the present time or at least slowing it down considerably.

It is probably very important to examine what factors seem to be insurmountable obstacles in policy development. One of the main factors seems to be a denial that there is a problem that needs solving (or an issue that needs addressing). Several interviewees said that their biggest obstacle was the attitude of many trustees and staff who refuse to acknowledge that racism exists or at least that there are systemic barriers to equality in education. Another major obstacle to policy development, once the issue is acknowledged, is lack of resources.

When boards are developing policy, however, they may feel that there are unique problems or situations in their areas that shape the way in which the particular policy is developed. These unique factors are listed in Table 14. The main clusters of factors are geographic and demographic. The perceived diversity of the community and the particular local characteristics are very important in the process of policy development. If a board perceives itself to be serving a homogeneous population, then there is less likelihood of interest in policy development for race and ethnocultural equity. North-South differences are also very important. Northern boards have created policies that acknowledge primarily the presence of aboriginal students. Small

TABLE 13

MAIN FACTORS THAT PREVENT SUCCESS OR ARE A BARRIER TO POLICY DEVELOPMENT (LISTED BY FREQUENCY)

BOARDS WITH POLICIES		BOARDS WITHOUT POLICIES	
5	Perception of No Racial Problems	5	No Problem in This Area
4	Lack of Resources	5	Not a Priority
1	Lack of Support	5	Lack of Time and Money
1	Putting All the Elements in One Document (Program, Employment, etc.)	4	Nature of the Community
1	Apathy	3	Provincial Legislation Needed
1	Political Will (1989)	3	Policy Not Needed
1	Having People Face Issues	2	Too Sensitive a Subject
1	More Negative Climate Today due to Proximity to Metro and Current Tensions	1	Provincial Legislation Not Needed for Enforcement (Would Cause Negative Reaction)
		1	Time and Pressure of Forming an FLI Board
		1	Arbitrary Development

TABLE 14

UNIQUE FACTORS TO BE TAKEN INTO CONSIDERATION WITH REGARDS
TO POLICY DEVELOPMENT (LISTED BY FREQUENCY)

BOARDS WITH POLICIES		BOARDS WITHOUT POLICIES	
4	Population is Enormously Multi-Ethnic	6	Small Ethnic Population
3	Little Immigration	4	Rural Community
3	Large and Fast Growing Population with Diverse Ethnic Groups	3	Geographic Location
2	Size	2	Distance Between Schools
2	Diverse Attitudes and Community Wide Geographical Variance in Demographic Make Up	2	Difference of Opinion Between North and South
2	Large Geographical Area	2	Strong Cultural and Religious Ties
1	Board Serves 5 Reserves	1	Cosmopolitan Population of School
1	Strong Feeling That Special Treatment is Wrong	1	Influx of New Canadians
1	Staffing - Location Makes It Difficult to Attract Minorities	1	Still a Very Homogeneous Population (WASP) - Only Recently Seeing Some Changes in Population
1	Complexity of the Administrative Structure	1	Small Staff
1	Border City to the USA	1	Inner City Board with Large Number of Immigrant Children
1	Nature of School Population	1	History of "Anglo' Loyalist" Dominates
1	Large Number of ESL/D Students		
1	Franco-Ontarion Community French Immersion		
1	Ottawa is the location of: Capital of Canada (Embassies) Secretary of State - Multiculturalism Ministry of Citizenship (Ontario)		
1	Board Serves 5 Reserves		

local clusters of immigrant workers and their families may also have programs developed specifically for them.

The awareness of locally available resources was also tapped in this survey. The findings are listed in Table 15. It was considered important to investigate whether school board personnel perceived that local resources were available to develop policy and to help with professional development activities. Once again, the boards with policies cite a wider network of resources of every kind. However, it is also noteworthy that boards without policies focus in on a rich variety of local resources that are available in rural and northern districts. In terms of networking, these boards are farther from large cities (or other cities), universities and resource centres. *New ways need to be devised to communicate with these areas.* However, this finding should not detract from the excellent use that is being made of local resources in some areas.

In an overall sense, boards were asked to state what were their highest priorities in the next five years, both in race and ethnocultural relations and in general. The findings are listed in Table 16. They show that boards with policies have specific goals in this area, whereas boards without policies are planning ways to start the process. Boards with policies are now planning to focus more specifically on implementation through affirmative action, in-service of teachers, and curriculum development. Boards without policies are still involved in the development stage.

TABLE 15

LOCAL RESOURCES FOR POLICY DEVELOPMENT OR
PROFESSIONAL DEVELOPMENT DAYS

	BOARDS WITH POLICIES		BOARDS WITHOUT POLICIES	
MINISTRY RELATED:	3	Ministry of Citizenship	3	Ministry of Citizenship
	2	Federal Government Department (Multiculturalism & Race Relations)		
	1	Embassies/High Commissions		
	1	Ontario Human Rights Commission		
	1	Race Relations Directorate		
SCHOOL RELATED:	5	Board Personnel	5	Board Resources Native Advisory
	3	School Staff		
	3	Race Relations Personnel		
	1	Heritage Language Teachers		
	1	Students		
COMMUNITY RELATED:	9	Local Multicultural Organizations	7	Multicultural Associations
	5	Ethnic Organizations	3	Native Friendship Centre
	3	Community Council	3	Organized Cultural Groups
	1	Human Rights Association	1	Band Counsellors
	1	YMCA	1	Folk Arts Council
	1	Social Agencies	1	Local Parishes
	1	Friendship Centre		
	1	Objibway-Cree Centre		
	1	Multicultural Groups		

TABLE 15 (Cont'd)

OTHER:
- 4 Universities
- 3 Colleges
- 2 Cross Cultural Communication Centre
- 1 Urban Alliance on Race Relations
- 1 Ontario Welcome House
- 1 Consultant Members

- 4 Universities/Colleges
- 2 Native Reserves
- 2 United Immigrant Services
- 2 Print & Media Resources

TABLE 16
BOARD'S HIGHEST PRIORITY IN NEXT FIVE YEARS

	BOARDS WITH POLICIES			BOARDS WITHOUT POLICIES	
RACE AND ETHNO-CULTURAL GOALS:	7	Firm Implementation of Policy	17	Develop Policy	
	6	Increase Sensitivity of Staff and Students	4	Staff Awareness and Implementation in our Curriculum	
	4	Staff Development, Student Awareness	3	Promote and Support Multicultural Environment	
	3	Attract Visible Minorities for Employment	2	Analysis of Ethnocultural Equity Within System	
	3	Continue Implementing of Staff and Students	2	Hiring and Promotional Practices	
	1	Curriculum for Multicultural Issues	2	Keep Improving Native Education	
	1	Develop Guidelines for Resolving Incidents	1	Too Early To Say	
	1	Reflect Gospel Values - Love for All	1	(Leadership, Curriculum, Awareness	
	1	Be Pro-Active in All Departments in Race Equity	1	Following the Goals of Education	
OTHER GOALS:	5	Responding to Curriculum Challenges	8	Responding to Growth	
	4	Improving Services in Era of Continual Growth	5	Facilities and Program Excellence	
	3	Create Climate for Implementation	5	Unknown at This Time	
	2	More Funding	3	Staffing and Recruitment and Leadership	
	1	Ethnic Programs and Relevant Experiences	3	No Concern	
	1	Transferable of Secondary School to MSSB (Metro Separate School Board)	2	Curriculum Development and Implementation	
	1	Review of Existing Policy	2	Active Learning	
	1	Raise Awareness	1	Establish and Effectively Implement a Policy	
	1	Provide Quality Education			
	1	Decentralization for More School-Based Planning			
	1	Employment Equity			

In regard to overall goals, the boards with policies are more likely to mention race and ethnocultural equity concerns as one of their highest priorities overall. In no case did a board without a policy mention race and ethnocultural equity concerns as an overall goal. This finding can be explained in two ways: boards with policies may serve a strikingly heterogeneous community and may see race and ethnocultural equity as a high priority or the process of race and ethnocultural equity policy development may have sensitized boards to concerns in this area. There is no doubt, however, that providing services in a time of fiscal constraint is one of the major concerns of all school boards. Curriculum and staff development are also major concerns. Interview data show clearly that for some boards race and ethnocultural equity is a major focus, whereas for others it is seen as quite tangential.

Francophone Issues

The following ten school boards were sent a letter and questionnaire by the Francophone research associate (See Appendix A3). This list is not exhaustive.

1. C.E.S.C.D. de Cochrane-Iroquois Falls
2. C.E.S.C.D. de Hearst
3. C.E.S.C.D. de Kapuskasing
4. C.S.L.F. d'Ottawa-Carleton
5. C.E.C. de Prescott-Russell
6. C.E. Comte Prescott-Russell
7. C.E.C. Stormont, Dundas, et Glengarry
8. C.E.S.C. de Sudbury
9. C.E.S. de Timmins
10. C.E.F.C.U. de Toronto

The boards in Toronto and Ottawa-Carleton are regional boards, and the other eight are French language sections of separate or public boards.

The only difference in the questionnaire was in question 5, where respondents were asked to list the major *linguistic*, racial, and ethnocultural minority groups served by their board (addition of the word *linguistic*). They were also give a telephone number to contact to speak to the Francophone researcher, and all of them were telephoned for a follow-up instead of being sent the letter.

The return rate on the questionnaire was 40%, with one board, Timmins R.C.S.S.B. noting that they had a policy, and three boards stating that they did not: Prescott, Dundas, Glengarry, Cochrane Iroquois Falls-Black River Matheson, Kapuskasing, and Ottawa-Carleton. Information was gathered in the telephone interviews on the other boards. The statistical information for the Francophone segment has all been included in the overall findings, but the distinctive differences are noted here. Basically, the ten telephone interviews form the basis for these findings.

It is of importance to note that the French-language sections of boards have usually been participants in the policy making of their English-speaking boards. Structurally or organizationally, they have not been expected to develop their own policies since they are perceived to be part of these boards. However, since some of the issues at stake are different for Francophones than for Anglophones, there is a general feeling among Francophones that there should be a distinct process of policy development for their sections of the boards.

The two regional boards (Ottawa-Carleton and Toronto) - created after Bill 75 in 1986 which followed the decision rendered by the Ontario Court of Appeal in 1984 and the adoption of the Canadian Charter of Rights and Freedoms in 1982 and which have all led to a greater degree of responsibility by the Franco-Ontarian community for French-language schools and programmes - are now in a position to develop such policies, particularly since in these boards exists a mixed ethnocultural and racial population. These two boards had so much to accomplish in the initial stages of their existence that they can hardly have found the time to develop policies. Both, the Toronto and the Ottawa-Carleton boards have officially been in place only since January 1989. In Ottawa-Carleton, the telephone interviews revealed much interest in policy development in both the public and separate sectors.

In Northern Ontario, the French-speaking sections of the boards were interested in the concept of a race and ethnocultural equity policy because of the aboriginal children attending their schools. In one case, it was reported that the board served entirely *canadiens-français pure laine* (French-Canadians born and bred).

In Southern Ontario, the French sections of boards serve a small-town or rural population that is relatively homogeneous, and in Toronto and Ottawa an urban population that is multicultural and multiracial.

The questionnaire results indicate a lack of overall policy on race and ethnocultural equity in most cases, and also a lack of supporting documents. Again, these results must be interpreted in the light of the organizational context mentioned above. Francophones are either part of bigger English-speaking boards or have just established their own boards.

Basically, school board personnel expressed the belief that the French population in Ontario is doubly or triply disadvantaged, and the boards or sections of boards have been so busy struggling for their own rights in the last two decades that they are only now turning their attention to matters of race and ethnocultural equity within the Franco-Ontarian context. Historically, they have been denied rights in education, and a whole generation of older Franco-Ontarians are largely poorly educated or illiterate because of the lack of provincial funding for distinct high schools until 1968. A large proportion of them have worked in service or manual occupations in Northern Ontario, and have suffered the disadvantage of region and language. The Franco-Ontarians in the South have become an invisible minority population in the cities, and have also experienced educational disadvantage.

In addition, school board personnel mentioned that the very interesting symbolic use of French made in English-speaking schools has meant that already privileged English speakers have increased their advantage by learning French (often from teachers of European or Quebec origin) in French Immersion courses. On the other hand, Franco-Ontarians have often attended schools in which they were perceived as a disadvantaged minority while being native speakers of a language that Anglophones can use to gain prestige!

To complicate matters further, particularly in Ottawa and Toronto, French schools are also attended by "allophones", (native speakers of neither English nor French as a mother tongue). Some school personnel interviewed considered that it was not the job of French school boards to provide a multicultural, multiracial environment for allophones, but given their own fragile minority position, to use their schools to further the position of Franco-Ontarians. In Ottawa-Carleton, however, classes in French as a second language are being offered to allophones in four high schools. Indeed immigrants who are racial minorities may have less difficulty identifying with Franco-Ontarians than do European immigrants of a higher social class. The question remains as to whether French schools are strong enough to gallicize newcomers.

Thus it can be seen that the struggle for language rights overshadows question of cultural or racial equity policy, since the integration of allophones implies the development of special programmes and therefore, the allocation of time, expertise and money. Competence in the French language becomes the decisive issue. Allophones become a problem, for the teaching staff especially, only insofar as they do not speak French. Therefore, a student of a different racial and ethnocultural background who speaks French would find it easier to be granted admission to French schools than one who does not speak French. There are students from many racial and ethnocultural backgrounds in the French sections of the public and separate boards. Yet the emphasis on French language and culture remains predominant, both at the level of ideology and program.

In a few cases, a committee has been formed on ethnocultural relations. However, for reasons explored above, very little interview data emerged about the process of policy development. The major debates that are going on in French school boards seem to be about resisting the tide of anglicization from English-speaking offspring of parents educated in French (who can be admitted to French schools under Section 23 of the Charter of Rights and Freedoms). However, it is interesting to note that strictly speaking children of parents educated in French in other countries (Haiti, Vietnam, Lebanon) are not constitutionally entitled to French education in Ontario. Most of them do form the racial minority population in French schools (in addition to the aboriginal children primarily in the North).

In conclusion, interviewees noted that the situation of French-speaking children in Ontario is changing. They are a new generation of offspring of educated Francophones, immigrants from Quebec, and immigrants from many other French-speaking countries of the world. There is a new consciousness of being a French speaker in Ontario, a consciousness aided in no small measure by the many improvements in services for French speakers in Ontario. The educational system is part of this process, and a concern for racial and ethnocultural equity will surely follow when the position of French speakers is secure.

Aboriginal Issues

The results of this survey can be interpreted with specific reference to issues that concern aboriginal peoples in Ontario, and to some extent northern communities in general. The findings of particular note are highlighted here.

First, while several northern boards have developed policies, the boards that are more likely to have race and ethnocultural relations policies are urban and southern. The question of whether aboriginal peoples are even perceived to be relevant to a race, ethnocultural, or multicultural policy is important to ask. Whereas new immigrants and visible minorities are perceived to be racial, ethnocultural or multicultural groups, the aboriginal students are not perceived as newcomers and thus not the focus of equity concerns. Indeed, in some northern communities it is visible minority immigrant persons who have drawn the issue to the attention of the school board, and aboriginal peoples have lent their support to this effort.

In other communities, it was the low achievement scores of aboriginal students that caused parents to request some form of program review or policy development. More specific charges of racial harassment by other students at school have sometimes led to a generally heightened level of awareness and subsequent action.

In general, boards with and without overall policies are equally likely to have support documents on native studies. However, boards without policies are far more likely to be in areas where aboriginal students are the largest minority group attending the schools. This finding holds true in both northern and southern boards. The factor of rural location seems to be the salient cross-cutting variable. Boards that are rural are less likely to have policies and more likely to have aboriginal students. In rural boards, there are fewer resources and less access to major urban centres.

The rural factor should not obscure a discussion of the needs of aboriginal students, but it is linked with it. For example, in some high schools in Northern Ontario, students have travelled many hundreds of kilometres from home, and are lodged in boarding situations. Sometimes their lodging has been arranged by the school board, and sometimes by the local band council. In any event, these students often feel less at home than their non-aboriginal peers and support services in guidance and programming have been provided in some cases for them.

In other cases, aboriginal children come with parents from remote areas and live in the town where the parents are taking up-grading or vocational courses. They then attend local schools where they are not familiar to the other children.

In both situations described above, the aboriginal students are perceived as migrant or transient, as there is a certain temporary quality to their stay. Just as the parents may not have social links in town, so also the children may lack the long-established ties that the other children may have. There is an eagerness in these situations among school board personnel to downplay the incidence of racial harassment, and aboriginal-white relations may be seen as a "problem".

On the other hand, in boards with a more multicultural perspective, aboriginal identities tend to be reflected in curriculum concerns, Native as a Second Language (NSL) Courses, or the hiring of native teachers. There is not a clear-cut distinction between these two approaches. However, in the former example, it would seem that boards with a "problem-oriented" view would find the process of policy development more distasteful, whereas in the latter, there are some more positive means of acknowledging aboriginal culture.

Critics can state that the multicultural approach is a palliative that makes aboriginal and non-aboriginal children alike feel happier at school, while having the objective of cultural assimilation of all groups as its goal. In some areas of the province, aboriginal parents have established their own schools for this reason. However, the point was raised in our interviews in the North that some aboriginal parents wanted their children educated in regular schools run by the local board because they wanted them to adapt to the town way of life and to be prepared for high school.

The fact of geography and distance in Northern Ontario means that students do travel large distances or move away from home to attend high school. There is a fact of cultural separation that occurs for aboriginal and non-aboriginal children alike. This is particularly acute when students travel to high school, and even more so to college or university. The relationship of the economy of Northern Ontario to the South also means that the non-aboriginal population of Northern Ontario tends to be psychologically oriented to the South, whereas many aboriginal people are oriented toward the North.

This division in geographic orientation causes distinct differences in attachment to the local environment and in aspirations for the future. Thus the very goals of education may seem different for various groups of students, and the peer relationships, particularly at the high school level, may reflect these different life situations.

The school administrators in Northern Ontario are part of a professional cadre who move to various parts of the province in the course of their duties. Thus some of them share the orientation and aspirations of the majority of the non-aboriginal students in their schools. This cultural similarity makes it more difficult to see the totally different perception that aboriginal people may have of the term "equity". They may not see high school education, or wage employment as the only worthwhile outcomes of childhood, but respect for the land and wildlife and a spiritual approach toward a different vision of life may be more important to them. Efforts to reflect these values in the curriculum of young children may seem more "equitable" than dealing with incidents of racial harassment. The whole area of value differences needs to be explored more fully, but some effort has been made here to explain why some boards are not perceived by aboriginal peoples to be providing their children with equitable treatment even if the system were "perfect" in non-aboriginal terms.

There is a great deal happening in the North that is outside the scope of this report, but education for aboriginal children has been provided via an enriched curriculum and an understanding of differing learning styles that is quite different from the experience of the last generation. However, many of the points raised here are still widely debated and have yet to be settled. The process of policy development itself, even if it is at a very slow pace, will set the stage for education of the next generation of aboriginal and non-aboriginal students in Northern Ontario.

The next section of this report amplifies the survey data by providing information based on the follow-up interviews that were done with key personnel from several boards which presently have policies.

INTERVIEWS ON POLICY DEVELOPMENT AND IMPLEMENTATION

Boards were asked to identify contact persons who could be interviewed in order to provide further insight into the processes leading to successful policy development and implementation, and the circumstances leading to variations in implementation in different school boards. Because of time constraints, a sample of school boards was selected from those that actually had policies in place. Interviews were conducted personally or by telephone with 43 contact people, representing 22 school boards in 10 cities. Visits were made to Windsor, Hamilton, London, Ottawa, Timmins, Parry Sound, Waterloo, and Metropolitan Toronto. The interview protocol can be found in Appendix B4.

Participants in this phase were frank in their assessment of how far their boards have progressed in implementation, and in their opinions of what were the key factors in success as well as the barriers to successful policy development and implementation. Neither the names of individuals interviewed nor their particular school boards are listed in order to maintain confidentiality.

Duration of the Process

The average time frame for policy development in this area, from creation of a committee or task force to its passing by the board of trustees, is at least 18 months to 2 years. Those boards that took significantly less time (i.e., less than a year) usually produced a one- or two-page list of policy statements with very little elaboration and no implementation procedures. Those who took significantly longer (i.e., three years or more) experienced difficulties because of changing staff and/or board of trustees, with changing priorities and procedures, had too large and unwieldy a committee, and/or had very complicated reporting procedures that acted as obstacles, with various hurdles to overcome at several levels of the system.

Beginning the Process

The interviews revealed that boards begin the process of policy development for one or a combination of three reasons:

a) general proactive action of senior officials and staff, sensitive to changing demographics and needs of students, community and staff;

b) political will of the board, usually prompted by one or two particularly assertive trustees, often after a conference or community meeting (see below);

c) a serious racial incident in a school, serving as a catalytic event to mobilize the community to put pressure on the board to have a policy.

"If we hadn't been to that conference ... we would probably not have developed a policy."

Several interviewers pointed to a particular meeting or conference as the catalyst that led to policy development in their board, particularly if the conference was attended by senior administrators (director and/or superintendents) or trustees.

Conferences were mentioned as serving two important purposes. First, they provide models from other boards that lead some administrators and trustees to feel that **their** board should be doing something too. Such conference participants often return to their own jurisdictions and set the process in motion for policy development. Both the joint ministry conference of March 1986 and the validation conferences in the fall of 1987 were mentioned in this context. As one interviewee put it:

> Both of the trustees were catalysts. After they attended the ministry conference in Toronto, they brought it to the Education Committee as a topic, established a subcommittee, and made a recommendation to the board.

Secondly, for those already involved in policy development and implementation, conferences provide valuable opportunities to network with people who are trying to do the same thing. Often, within a board, a consultant or teacher can feel very isolated or alone in shouldering the responsibility for policy implementation. Conferences forge ties for information sharing and moral support for continuing the struggle at home, in a field that is fraught with frustrations and that can make consultants or teachers very unpopular among their colleagues and vulnerable to their superiors. Networking meetings in the Central Region and in Metropolitan Toronto as well as more recently in the Western Region (London, Windsor) in collaboration with the Race Relations Directorate were cited as valuable in this regard, as were the annual conference and seminars of the Ontario Multicultural Association (OMAMO) and conferences and meetings hosted by school boards where others were invited.

The Committee/Task Force

The reason for starting the process of policy development appears to influence the size and composition of the committee, the role of the community, and the probability of an effective implementation strategy. Those boards who begin the process as a proactive measure in response to changing demographics and student needs tend to create average-sized committees (approx. 7-15) consisting primarily of staff members, and implementation is often inconsistent when the key players change (e.g., shift in superintendent or consultant). While the policy statements are lofty and well-worded, often neither accountability nor specific implementation and monitoring procedures to ensure change are built in. In cases where the motivation is proactive and staff-driven, but where outside experts and some experienced community members are involved, there is a much greater chance of implementation procedures, accountability, and monitoring mechanisms being built into the policy.

Policies that are trustee-driven are usually developed by smaller committees (3-7 members on average) including a few trustees and selected staff members. While such policies are usually adopted readily by the board of trustees, there is the necessity of a lengthy "selling" phase for staff, and implementation, unless well-planned, is difficult.

Committees tend to be larger (although one board had 5 members, the range otherwise was 10-40 with the average 15) for boards where the community pressured for change as a result of a catalytic (racial) incident or series of incidents. The presence of community members or representatives of outside agencies (e.g., Ontario Human Rights Commission, Race Relations Directorate, Municipal Race Relations Committee, Ministry of Citizenship) tends to make the process take longer, but ensures a diversity of opinions and usually results in a monitoring procedure being put in place, along with accountability of senior officials.

The optimal size and structure for an effective working committee appears to be 7 to 15 members, including representatives of the trustees, senior administration, principals' association, teachers' federations, related specialty areas (e.g., ESL, Heritage Languages, student services), as well as a few community representatives of recognized organizations (e.g., Urban Alliance on Race Relations, Ontario Multicultural Association, local ethnocultural groups or Multicultural Council, Native Friendship Centre) and/or representatives of outside agencies specializing in race and ethnocultural issues as described above (OHRC, RRD), municipal committee, etc.

The most effective structure appears to include a chair or co-chair from the senior administration (i.e., the director or a superintendent) or at least a chair who reports directly to the director if his or her position is below that of a superintendent.

Role of the Community

Every person interviewed cited community involvement as essential to the process of policy development, although the exact role of the community differed significantly from board to board depending on two factors: 1) committee structure and function, and 2) levels of awareness and organization of the community.

As was mentioned above, boards who put the process in motion as a result of community pressure were more likely to include the community on the policy development committee and in the validation process, although all boards interviewed did involve the community in the validation process, even if they did not seek input prior to or during the development phase. The more organized the local communities are, the more aware they are of the processes of the board and of effective lobbying strategies. It was not unusual to hear of organized presentations to the board and packed boardrooms on the nights that the policy was being considered. The most effective role of the community in terms of implementation appears to be a monitoring role that evolves out of a partnership approach during the development phase. Boards who use this approach cite community involvement as a key factor in success; boards for whom community relations have been hostile on these issues cite community involvement as a barrier to successful implementation because of negative feelings among staff. In such situations, a facilitator who can play a mediating role was found to be helpful. Also committees who themselves underwent an educative process or in-service training on key issues experienced less conflict and developed more of a partnership approach.

Resources Used

Most boards used primarily internal resources for policy development, including release time for meetings, secretarial support, and budget for the amenities of lengthy committee work (e.g., dinners, retreats). Local community resources were used frequently, particularly in terms of representatives from minority groups coming in to give information sessions. Clearly boards in large urban centres have access to many outside resources, and they used them frequently, the most helpful being human resources (consultants, trainers, personnel from other boards, experts from government and community agencies). Several interviewees cited the importance of financial resources to purchase materials and services. Although some boards managed to access grant money (e.g. from the Ministry of Citizenship or the Secretary of State), the consensus appears to be that the application procedure is long and tedious and often not worth the effort. Those boards who appeared most successful in policy development **and** implementation are those in which the board (senior administration) reallocated existing funds to provide sufficient internal resources (time, money, support staff) to facilitate the process.

While the northern and rural boards appear to be somewhat limited in availability of both financial and human resources for policy development and implementation in this area, it was the consensus among those interviewed from the larger southern and urban boards that **if** race and ethnocultural equity is really a priority of the board, then funds do not appear to be a problem. If it is **not** a priority, then lack of funds becomes a stumbling block (or used as one by those who have the decision-making power on resource allocation).

Key Factors in Success: Development Phase

>The key factor for success in policy development was the leadership of senior officials in the board.

Without exception, all boards interviewed cited support **and commitment of senior administration** as a key factor in successful policy development **and** implementation. Whether the impetus for development came from trustees or community, the supervisory officers were seen as the key element in the success or failure of putting policy into practice. Their involvement in the process leads to ownership that is essential. As one interviewee put it:

>The key factor is the administration. If it is just a political process, it will fail. Each has to believe it in his heart and soul.

Also, without exception, **community involvement** was listed as a key factor in success in the development stage. This takes the form of input prior to or during the committee's work, and also participation in the validation process. Several people mentioned the importance of effective outreach to the community so that the board is perceived as genuine. For example, invitations to the community to respond to anything should allow enough **time**, given that organizations usually meet only once a month. And going out to the community enhances access, as opposed to expecting the community always to come to the board. When community members do come to the board, it is essential to provide a credible forum, where they are listened to by people in authority and where they can believe they are being heard.

Attitudes and values of the board (trustees and staff) were often cited as a key factor in successful policy development - and also a main barrier to implementation if those attitudes are negative. On the positive side, one interviewee highlighted the attitude of the board in this way:

> For us the key factor in success was a common desire to show that the board cares about this because we do not want students to suffer from discrimination. We need to know how to deal with it.

On the reverse side, the attitudes of several key people in the board were seen as major obstacles to policy development and implementation. A few people interviewed said that the most difficult barrier to success was the reluctance of people to admit that racism exists in the society and the school system, and a total lack of understanding of the issues.

Where they were used, **outside resource people** were consistently cited as a key factor in successful policy development. Private consultants/facilitators, representatives of government agencies, consultants and resource people from other boards, were all seen as extremely useful in facilitating the process.

Representatives of one board summarized the four key factors in success as follows:

- an outside facilitator who found ways of solving the differences
- it was a working committee with commmunication with the community
- the Task Force members were committed people who really believed in what they were doing
- the director chaired the committee.

Key Factors in Success: Implementation Phase

Again, the support and commitment of the **senior administration** was seen by all those interviewed as an essential ingredient for successful policy implementation.

When **responsibilities** of senior officials are clearly spelled out and **accountability** built into the policy and procedures, then the probability of effecting change is **greatly** enhanced. Boards that have had their policies in place long enough to have undergone a review, found consistently that failure to specify lack of responsibility and accountability was a major barrier to policy implementation.

The importance of a monitoring mechanism in the form of a board committee or an advisory committee to the director (i.e., a committee with some **clout and community representation**) was listed as a key factor in successful policy implementation. Where such committees are weak, have an unclear mandate, little or no community involvement and must report through several levels before getting to the director and board, implementation is slow and, in some cases, non-existent.

Staff **attitudes, values, and priorities** again were cited as key factors in success (or barriers to) policy implementation. Where attitudes are negative and there is resistance to the policy and proposed changes, it is not politically wise to be overt in one's resistance; but covert strategies are used to block implementation. For example, it may take months for certain issues to appear on the agenda of a key committee; or the consultant may be told that "this is not the way we do it here", or "there are no funds available"; or resources may be cut back in the department to only a half-time secretary; or where other departments are expanding, the race relations position may be combined with another portfolio, or the workshop on Race and Ethnocultural Equity may be placed opposite "Planning Your Retirement", "Exchange Trips to Europe", and "Everything You Ever Wanted to Know about Teaching Junior Math" on Federation Day, with no other professional development opportunities for two years! There are many ways to impede progress in this area when it is not a priority of the decision makers.

There is no doubt that what the participants in the interview phase saw as key factors in successful implementation would increase anxiety, tension and feelings of territoriality among those staff members for whom the race and ethnocultural equity policy is threatening (because they fear loss of power) or who are opposed to the concepts because of lack of awareness, understanding, or perhaps even bigotry and racism.

Almost all of those interviewed highlighted the importance of effective **in-service training at all** levels of the system. In boards where the most progress had been made in implementation (including effective procedures for handling racial incidents, change in employment practices, curriculum development and implementation, effective assessment procedures, improved school/community relations), compulsory in-service had begun with senior administration and included all principals and persons in supervisory positions of any kind. In boards where implementation was slow or even totally ineffective, senior officials "did not have time" to attend in-service sessions or have these topics as the focus of their retreat. Superintendents who are held responsible and accountable for policy implementation have found the time.

Where implementation is underway, in-service sessions are also given to school support staff (secretaries, custodians, bus drivers) as well as central office staff and consultants, librarians, psychology services, and so on - in collaboration with the relevant departments.

> "We had a workshop by the Multicultural Association for principals, many of whom suffered from the 'Ostrich Syndrome'."

In one board where policy implementation is well underway, **all** principals attend a series of workshops on community/school relations and handling racial incidents. In another, a ten-week course is offered to principals and attended by many. In yet another board, where there are barriers to implementation, the consultant was told he could not get the principals to do anything and was wished luck in trying ... on his own.

All those interviewed agreed that **adequate** budget was essential for effective policy implementation. Boards cannot conduct reasonable in-service programs or in-school initiatives or provide resources to teachers without financial resources. Many boards are looking to the ministry to provide the necessary funds where resources are short. Others are using outside funding sources where available and where they have skills in obtaining grants. Several others (where implementation is most successful) prefer to work through supportive senior officials for resource reallocation, so that programs for race and ethnocultural equity are put right into the corporate plan, become entrenched in the system and not dependent on "soft money" which can be cut back or cut off completely.

It seems clear from the interviews that another key factor in success of policy implementation is a **staff person** charged with facilitating implementation who is committed, energetic, personable, and politically astute, who has extensive knowledge and skill in the areas of multiculturalism, ethnic and race relations, is a team player, a risk taker, has awareness and understanding of the processes of organizational development and change ... and has the support of his/her director and superintendent.

Notice that the role should be one of **facilitating** implementation. If the designated staff person is viewed as the one to actually implement the policy single-handedly, that person will likely burn out or move on, leaving little evidence of policy implementation. Boards that are serious about implementing a policy on race and ethnocultural equity provide a structure that has a greater chance of success by putting in place the key factors identified above.

SUMMARY AND CONCLUSIONS

The purpose of this study was to gather all race and ethnocultural equity policies in school boards and to analyze their development and implementation with a view to making some recommendations to the Ministry of Education for further action. The overall goal of the study has been achieved. With such a high response rate to the survey (100 out of 124 or 80.6%) the results present a clear picture of the "state of the art" of policy development and implementation in school boards across the province. In general, it may be concluded that:

- 39 boards have policies, 3 have drafts that are nearly completed, and 22 boards are in the process of developing a policy;

- these policies are considered to be different from other policies because of the nature of their content and pervasiveness of outcomes;

- they take longer to develop than other policies (average 18 months to 2 years);

- they usually involve community input and validation and monitoring;

- the entire system is (or should be) affected by these policies;

- there is often tremendous resistance to overcome in policy development and implementation; this resistance may be obvious or covert;

- responsibility and accountability must be built into the policy to ensure implementation;

- staff responsible for these policies are often vulnerable, must take risks, and need real and moral support to reduce stress and enhance efficiency;

- several school boards in the province have created policies that have effectively acknowledged the concerns of native parents and students, particularly in curriculum and guidance; however, many school boards have not yet perceived that the needs of native students should be addressed in a policy of race and ethnocultural equity;

- school boards feel they need additional financial and human resources or resource reallocation to develop and implement policies in this area;

- there are useful resources and resource people available throughout the province, but knowledge about them needs to be disseminated and shared through networking and funding;

- the content, format, structure, and language of policies vary widely and will have to be standardized somewhat to ensure equity for all Ontarians, but appropriate for specific areas and needs;

- in-service training is viewed as essential for all staff, trustees and committee members to enhance policy development and implementation.

In addition to the findings above, participants highlighted several other factors, namely the importance of policy in this area, the role of the senior administrators and decision makers, the role of the community, the language used, and the need for further research. These will be elaborated below.

The Importance of Policy

While it might be said that a built-in bias in the data exists because boards **with** policies were the most vocal in this study, nevertheless the responses consistently emphasized the importance of such policies being entrenched at the very core of school administration. Where there **are** policies, things happen; where there **are not**, they do not. Therefore, it may be concluded from this study that if the Province of Ontario wants to achieve race and ethnocultural equity in education for all Ontarians, it follows that the Ministry of Education should **mandate** policy in this area for **all** school boards.

Role of Administrators

In view of the importance attached to the attitude and support of the supervisory officers in both policy development and implementation (virtually every respondent mentioned this as a key factor in success), more work must be done with senior administrators to prepare them for their role in this area. Compulsory components on multiculturalism, ethnic and race relations should be in all courses for supervisory officers and principals. Compulsory up-grading courses should be in place for supervisory officers and principals to provide in-service training on race and ethnocultural equity, including material on achieving employment equity, performance review procedures, handling racial incidents, assessment and placement, and school/community relations. It should be noted that, according to the findings of this study, should ministry or board officials or decision makers respond to this conclusion with references to the lack of precedent, or "this is not how it is done in the ministry", or "there is no time or money for this", then that could be construed as a lack of priority and commitment, and a barrier to successful policy development and implementation.

Role of the Community

It may be concluded from this study that in order to maximize the effectiveness of policy development and implementation for race and ethnocultural equity, the community must be involved at several stages - input, validation, and monitoring and evaluation of implementation. Effective guidelines should be prepared for school boards to enhance school/community relations through partnerships to avoid their being on opposite sides of this issue at the political level, and to ensure the community feels the board is genuine and is prepared to listen (and to hear) their needs and concerns.

The Language of Equity

Another conclusion can be drawn in terms of the underlying philosophy as reflected by terminology used. Most people prefer the concept of "equity" as the overall goal of the policy. The term "anti-racist education" was used spontaneously only by people interviewed who also happened to have served on the provincial advisory committee. Most others consistently used the term "race relations" or "multiculturalism" in addition to "race and ethnocultural equity". As one interviewee put it:

"The anti-racist approach does not say what people are for, only against. Race and ethnocultural equity in education sets the tone ... is more positive."

It may be concluded that a positive, practical approach to achieving race and ethnocultural equity will achieve the goals of anti-racist education without exascerbating the situation by using language that connotes conflict. The findings indicate that if a school board is interested in effecting change, it must use strategies and language to move people along in the right direction, not to increase resistance.

Need for Research

While there is a distinct shortage of research in this area, boards that are implementing policies recognize the importance of collecting data to monitor change. Until now, evaluation of change has been primarily subjective, although interpretation of objective data may lead to different conclusions and vice versa. These two quotes from the interviews illustrate this point:

"We can evaluate the success of implementation in two ways: there has been a **decrease** in the frequency of reporting racial incidents; and there has been a noticeable affective component - more smiles and warmth."

"I can tell the policy is successful. People are feeling more confident now, so there is an **increase** in the number of reported racial incidents, because people are now coming forward, whereas before they were not."

Both the literature review and the interview data revealed that there were many opinions on what **should** be done to change students and staff attitude and behaviour, there is very little documented evidence on the most effective methods of doing so and on the impact of policy. There is clearly a need for good quality Canadian research in this area.

RECOMMENDATIONS FOR ACTION

The results of the survey and interviews across the province suggest the following recommendations for action to move towards race and ethnocultural equity in schools:

1. In order for the development and implementation of policies and procedures for race and ethnocultural equity to become a priority among school boards, the ministry should make such policies **mandatory**, including responsibilities and accountability.

2. Clear **guidelines** for policy development and implementation should be made available, and sufficient resources allocated to enable all boards to develop and implement policies effectively, according to provincial standards and also according to their particular needs and context.

3. **Information** on existing policies and support documents should be made available in a format that is easily accessible to every board in the province.

4. Local **resource centres** should be set up by the ministry in each region to provide a clearinghouse of information, specialized resource collections, and local speakers and resource persons for workshops, committees, and task forces.

5. The Ministry of Education should assist the regions to set up **networks** of personnel involved in policy development and implementation, to share information and resources and provide the outside support necessary for effective work in this area.

6. **A policy development manual** should be developed, based on the results of this study, to present various models of policy development and practical step-by-step guidelines on implementation. Sections should be included on francophone and native issues, and how to involve the community effectively.

7. The Government of Ontario should **allocate funds** to enable the Ministry of Education to assist school boards through a system of grants to develop policy and implementation procedures since effective policy development requires sufficient time and the commitment (and release time) of various staff members,

as well as a level of support for the process that can put a strain on smaller boards with fewer resources.

8. Funds should be made available to **conduct research** on the efficacy of policy and procedures in effecting change in social attitudes and behaviour in children of various ages in schools, as well as research on employment practices in school boards.

9. Since many school boards are looking to the Ministry of Education for **leadership and guidance** in this area, the basic tenets of race and ethnocultural equity should be practiced by the ministry itself. That is, the ministry should conduct a review of internal policies practice and programs within its purview so as to develop and implement procedures to achieve race and ethnocultural equity. These would include:

- enhancing the curriculum of all **ministry courses** (especially those for supervisory officers and principals) to include adequate preparation in this area;

- developing **employment policies and procedures** to eliminate barriers to equality in employment within the ministry;

- providing **in-service training** to all ministry personnel to enhance their awareness, understanding, and skills in managing and valuing diversity;

- providing intensive training to all **education officers** with responsibilities for race relations, so that they can provide resources, leadership, and guidance in the regions;

- establishing **criteria** for **evaluation and monitoring** of policy development and implementation;

- **funding research** and providing incentives both in the ministry and in school boards to determine the effectiveness of policy development in effecting change in all areas addressed by the policies;

- including knowledge and experience in race and ethnocultural equity issues as **requirements for teacher certification** in the Province of Ontario.

10. In the carrying out of all the above recommendations, particular attention should be paid to the interests and concerns of school boards serving **native** and **francophone** populations.

RACE AND ETHNOCULTURAL EQUITY IN EDUCATION:

SURVEY OF POLICY DEVELOPMENT AND IMPLEMENTATION

RESOURCE BIBLIOGRAPHY

RESOURCE BIBLIOGRAPHY

The following bibliography is organized to correspond to the major sections presented in the *Survey of Race and Ethnocultural Policy Development and Implementation in Ontario Schools*. Suggested background materials are included for curriculum development, assessment and placement, employment and staff development, children and racism, school community relations, and a general ethnocultural resource section. An annotated section is included for a literature review on handling racial incidents and discrimination in schools. While there is some literature on the development of racial awareness and attitudes in young children and suggested strategies for creating an anti-racist school environment, there is a distinct shortage of Canadian research on and documentation of equity issues in school situations with regards to age groups, mechanisms in place, and current and future needs. It is important to identify both the causes and effects of conflict and stereotyping as they affect various age groups in schools in order to provide a reliable basis of information as a foundation on which to bring about change for equity.

1. CURRICULUM DEVELOPMENT

Baker, Gwendolyn C. (1983). *Planning and Organizing for Multicultural Instruction.* Toronto: Addison Wesley.

Banks, James A. (1981). *Multiethnic Education: Theory and Practice.* Boston: Allyn and Bacon Inc.

Burke, M.E. and Fraser, K. (1981) *Home Base Strategies for Teaching Human Rights in Ontario Classrooms: Curriculum Ideas for Teachers* (Intermediate and Senior). Toronto: Ontario Human Rights Commission, 32 p (pending publication).

Butt, R.L. (1989). Twenty-five criteria for the design of multicultural education materials: a needs-based approach. *Multiculturalism*, vol. 12, 9-15.

De Vries, D.L., Edwards, K.J. and Slavin, R.E. (1978). Biracial learning teams and race relations in the classroom: Four field experiments using Teams-Games-Tournament. *Journal of Educational Psychology*, 70, 356-362.

Farrell, Lennox (1988). Report on streaming in education neglects black community needs. *Now*, March, 17-23.

Haughton, Harry S. (Dr.) (1987). *Children Smile in the Same Language: Songs for Multiculturalism and Anti-Racism Education.* Mississauga: Mississauga Publications and Resources in Education and the Social Services.

Hicks, D. (1981). *Minorities: A Teachers Resource Book for the Multi-Ethnic Curriculum.* London: Heinemann.

Kehoe, J. (1984). *A Handbook for Enhancing the Multicultural Climate of the School.* Vancouver: Western Education Development Group.

Kehoe, J. and Perkins E. (1983). Experimental classroom activities for developing positive human rights attitudes. *Multiculturalism*, vol. 6, no. 2, 8-10.

Lee, Enid (1985). *Letters to Marcia: a Teachers Guide to Anti-racist Education.* Toronto: Cross-Cultural Communications Centre.

McLeod, Keith A. (Ed.) (1984). *Multicultural Early Childhood Education.* Toronto: University of Toronto Guidance Centre.

Ontario Ministry of Education (1983). *Black Studies.* Toronto: the ministry.

Samuda, R.J. and Kong, S.L. (Eds.) (1986). *Multicultural Education Programmes and Methods.* Toronto: Intercultural Social Sciences Publications, Inc.

Shiman, David A. (1979). *The Prejudice Book: Activities for the Classroom.* Toronto: Anti-Defamation League of B'nai Brith.

Tiedt, P.L. and Tiedt, I.M. (1979). *Multicultural Teaching: A Handbook of Activities, Information, and Resources.* Boston: Allyn and Bacon.

Tomlinson, Heather (1988). Tackling racism through the curriculum: an anti-racist exercise. *Multicultural Teaching*, vol. 7, no. 1, winter.

Urban Alliance on Race Relations (1979). *Growing Together: Programme Ideas for Children's Groups to Help them Grow into a Multi-Racial Community*. Toronto: the Alliance.

2. ASSESSMENT AND PLACEMENT OF STUDENTS

Cummins, J. (1984). *Bilingualism and Special Education: Issues in Assessment and Pedagogy*. San Diego, CA: College-Hill Press.

Cummins, J. (1986). Empowering minority students: A framework for intervention. *Harvard Education Review*, 56, 18-36.

Cummins, J. (1987). Psychological assessment in multicultural school systems. *Canadian Journal for Exceptional Children*, 3, 115-117.

Hoopes, D.S., Pederson, P.B. and Renwick, G.W. (Eds.) (1978). *Overview of Intercultural Education, Training and Research. Vol. II: Education and Training*. Washington, D.C.: SIETAR.

Ramcharan, S. (1975). Special Problems of Immigrant Children in Toronto. In A. Wolfgang (Ed.), *Education of the Immigrant Students*. Toronto: The Ontario Institute for Studies in Education.

Rogow, S. (1987). Children Who are Culturally Different. In M. Winger, S. Rogow, and C. David, *Exceptional Children in Canada*. Scarborough, Ontario: Prentice Hall.

Samuda, R. and Wolfgang, A. (Eds.) (1985). *Intercultural counselling and assessment*. Toronto: Hogrefe.

Samuda, R. (1975). *Psychological testing of American minorities*. New York: Harper and Row.

Samuda, R.J. and Crawford, D.H. (1980). *Testing, assessment, counselling and placement of ethnic minority students*. Toronto: Ontario Ministry of Education.

Samuda, R. and Tingling W. (1980). *The use of tests in the education of Canadian immigrants: building on strengths and deficits*. Kingston: Queen's University Press.

3. EMPLOYMENT AND STAFF DEVELOPMENT
(including Teacher Education)

Abella, R. (1984). *Royal Commission on Equality in Employment.* Ottawa: Government of Canada.

Allen, Jane (1988). *Employment Equity: How We Can Use It to Fight Racism.* Toronto: Cross-Cultural Communication Centre.

Armour, Monica (1984). *Visible Minorities: Invisible.* Toronto: Urban Alliance on Race Relations.

Ashworth, Mary (1979). *The Forces Which Shaped Them.* Vancouver, B.C.: New Star Books.

Canada. Multiculturalism (1985). *Cross Cultural Awareness Education and Training for professionsals: a Manual / La sensibilisation interculturelle : guide de formation des professionels.* Ottawa: Government of Canada.

Casse, Pierre (1981). *Training for the Cross-Cultural Mind.* 2nd ed. Washington, D.C.: SIETAR.

Central de l'Enseignement du Quebec (1983). *Si vous croyez aux droits humains : cahier pédagogique.* Québec : le Central.

Chanda, Mutale and Cook, P. (Ed.) (1986). *Workplace Discrimination: A Course for Supervisors, Foremen and Forewomen.* Toronto: Equal Opportunity Division Management Services Department.

Cheng, Maisy, L. (1987). *Visible Minority Representation in the Toronto Board of Education Staff Changes, 1986.* Toronto: Board of Education, Information Services Division.

Cheng, Maisy, L. (1987). *Who Seeks the Work? A Pre-employment Pilot Survey.* Toronto: Board of Education, Information Services Division.

Cheng, Maisy, L. (1987). *Representation of Visible/Racial Minorities in the Toronto Board of Education Work Force, 1987 Part I.* Toronto: Board of Education, Information Services Division.

Cheng, Maisy, L. (1988). *Representation of Visible/Racial Minorities in the Toronto Board of Education Work Force, 1987, Part II.* Toronto: Board of Education, Information Services Division.

Damen, Louise (1987). *Culture Learning: the Fifth Dimension in the Language Classroom.* Addison-Wesley.

Fantini, Alvino, E. (Ed.) (1984). *Beyond the Language Classroom: a Guide for Teachers.* Vermont: The Experiment in International Living.

Henley, Richard and Young, Jonathan (1989). Multicultural teacher education: part 3, curriculum content and curriculum structure. *Multiculturalism*, vol. 12, no. 1, 24-27.

Kehoe, J. (1981). Effective Tools for Combating Racism in the Schools. *Multiculturalism*, vol. 4, no. 3, 3-10.

Kehoe, J. (1983). Strategies for Human Rights Education. In D. Ray and V. Doyley (Eds.), *Human Rights in Canadian Education*. Dubuque, Iowa: Kendall/Hunt, 68-109.

Kehoe, J. (1984). *A Handbook for Enhancing the Multicultural Climate of the School*. Vancouver: Western Education Development Group, University of British Columbia.

Kehoe, J. & Perkins, E. (1983). Experimental Classroom Activities for Developing Positive Human Rights Attitudes. *Multiculturalism*, vol. 6, no. 2, 8-10.

Mallea, J. and Young, J. (1980). Teacher education for a multicultural society. In K. McLeod (Ed.), *Intercultural Education and Community Development*. Faculty of Education, University of Toronto, 87-93.

Masemann, V. and Mock K.R. (1987). *Multicultural Teacher Education in Canada*. Ottawa: Secretary of State, Multiculturalism Canada.

Mayes, N.H. and Commenou, C. (1978). Teacher education for cultural awareness. In Hoopes, Pederson and Renwick, (Eds), *Overview of Intercultural Education, Training and Research*. Volume II: *Education and Training*. Washington, D.C.: SIETAR.

McCreath, Peter (Ed.) (1981). *Multiculturalism: A Handbook for Teachers*. Halifax: Nova Scotia's Teacher's Union.

Mock, Karen R. (1983). The successful multicultural teacher. *The History and Social Science Teacher*, vol. 19, no. 2, 87-97.

Mock, Karen (1985). *Multicultural Preschool Education: a Resource Manual for Supervisors and Volunteers (ECE/ESL)*. Toronto: Ontario Ministry of Citizenship and Culture, Newcomer Services Branch.

Myers, J. and Taylor, M. (1983). Co-operative Techniques in the Classroom. *Multiculturalism*, vol. 1, no. 3, 7-10.

Pusch, Margaret. (1981). *Multicultural Education: a Cross Cultural Training Approach*. Chicago: Intercultural Press Inc.

Ray, D. (1980). Multiculturalism in teacher education. In K. McLeod (Ed.), *Intercultural Education and Community Development*. Faculty of Education, University of Toronto, 79-86.

Saracho, Olivia N. and Spodek, Bernard (Eds.) (1983). *Understanding the Multicultural Experience in Early Childhood Education*. Washington: National Association for the Education of Young Children.

Savvides, S. (1988). Problems in implementing a multiethnic education policy. The findings of a study of teachers' attitudes towards the implementation of multicultural education. *Multicultural Teaching*, vol. 7, no. 1, Winter 1988.

Slavin, R.E. and Madden, N.A. (1979). School practices that improve race relations. *American Educational Research Journal*, 16, 169-180.

Tsuji, Gerry J. (1986). *Visible Minority Representation in Toronto Board of Education Staff Changes, 1985.* Toronto: Board of Education, Information Services Branch.

Wolfgang, Aaron (Ed.) (1975). *Education of Immigrant Students: Issues and Answers.* Toronto: The Ontario Institute for Students in Education.

Wyatt, Beynon, J. (1985). Teacher preparation for the multiethnic classroom: reflective writing and attitude change. *Canadian Ethnic Studies*, vol. 17, no. 1, 34-50.

4. CHILDREN AND RACISM

Aboud, Frances (1988). *Children and Prejudice.* New York: Basil Blackwell Inc.

Aboud, Frances, E. (1977). Interest in ethnic information: a cross-cultural development study. *Canadian Journal of Behavioral Science*, 9, 134-136.

Adair, D. and Rosenstock, J. (1976). *Multiculturalism in the Classroom: A Survey of Interracial Attitudes in Ontario.* Toronto: Secretary of State Canada.

Allen, Sheila. (1979). Preschool children: ethnic minorities in England. *New Community*, 8, 135-142.

Ashworth, Mary (1978). *Immigrant Children and Canadian Schools.* Toronto: McClelland and Stewart Ltd.

Banks, J.A. and Grambs, J.D. (1982). *Black Self Concept.* New York: McGraw Hill.

Brand, Dionne and Sri Bhaggiyadatta, Krisantha (1986). *Rivers have Sources, Trees have Roots: Speaking of Racism.* Toronto: Cross Cultural Communication Centre.

Brown, R. (1979). Children and racism. *Multiculturalism*, vol. 3, no. 2.

Canada. Ministry of Supply and Services (1985). *Program of Action for the Second Decade to Combat Racism and Racial Discrimination.* Ottawa: Multiculturalism Canada.

Corenblum, B. and Annis, R.C. (1987). Racial identity and preference in Native and White Canadian children. *Canadian Journal of Behavioural Science*, 19, 254-65.

Crooks, R.C. (1970). The effects of an interracial preschool program upon racial preference, knowledge of racial differences and racial identification. *Journal of Social Issues*, 26, 137-44.

Doyle, A.B., Beaudet, J., and Aboud, F.E. (in press). Developmental patterns in the flexibility of children's ethnic attitudes. *Journal of Cross-Cultural Psychology.*

Fourth R. (1984). Racism and Education. *Currents: Readings in Race Relations*, vol. 2, no. 3, Fall.

Goodman, M.E. (1964). *Race Awareness in Young Children.* New York: Collier.

Hunsberger, B. (1978). Racial awareness and preference of White and Indian Canadian children. *Canadian Journal of Behavioural Science*, 10, 176-9.

Ijaz, Ahmed M. and Ijaz, Helene I. (1981). A cultural program for changing racial attitudes. *The History and Social Science Teacher*, vol. 17, no. 1, 17.

Kalin, R. (1979). Ethnic and multicultural attitudes among children in a Canadian city. *Canadian Ethnic Studies*, 11, 64-81.

Kehoe, J. and Echols, F. (1983). The effects of reading historical and contemporary cases of discrimination on attitudes toward selected minority groups. *Canadian Ethnic Studies*, vol. 15, no. 2, 92-105.

Laferrière, Michel (1982). Blacks in Quebec - minorities among minorities. *Research in Race and Ethnic Relations*, 3, 3-27.

Lee, M. (1983). Multiculturalism: education perspectives for the 1980's. *Education*, vol. 103, no. 4, 405-409, summer.

Lewis, M. (1983). Children's picture books: native Canadians and bias. *Dev/Ed News*, spring 8-10.

Manitoba. Human Rights Commission (1982). *Racism in Winnipeg Schools.* Winnipeg: Human Rights Commission.

Milner, David (1975). *Children and Race.* London: Penguin.

Moodley, Kogila (1984). The ambiguities of multicultural education. *Currents: Readings in Race Relations*, vol. 2, no. 3, fall.

Preiswerk, Roy (Ed.) (1980). *The Slant of the Pen: Racism in Children's Books.* Geneva: World Council of Churches.

Tator, Carol (1988). Anti-racist education. *Currents: Readings in Race Relations*, vol. 4, no. 4, winter, 8-11.

Thornhill, Esmeralda (1984). Fighting racism starting with schools. *Currents: Readings in Race Relations*, vol. 2, no. 3, fall.

5. SCHOOL AND COMMUNITY RELATIONS

Burke, M.E. (1982). The Ontario multicultural multiracial leadership camp: a residential learning experience. *Multiculturalism*, vol. 6, no. 1, 21-24.

Elliston, I.N. (1984). Multicultural Centres: A Focus for Intercultural Education In R. Samuda et al. (Eds.), *Multiculturalism in Canada: Social and Educational Perspectives*. Toronto: Allyn & Bacon, 309-326.

Masemann, V., Mock, K.R., and Lowe, K. (1988). *Access to Education: a manual for community groups*. Ottawa: Multiculturalism Canada, Secretary of State.

McLeod, K.A. (Ed.) (1980). *Intercultural Education and Community Development*. Toronto: University of Toronto Guidance Centre, Faculty of Education.

Palmer, Howard (1975). *Immigration and the Rise of Multiculturalism*. Toronto: Copp Clark Publishing.

Rees, Tim (Ed.) (1985). Race Relations and Municipal Government, *Currents*, vol. 3, no. 1. Toronto: Urban Alliance on Race Relations.

Sangha, D. (1983). The Vancouver neighbourhood action project: a community response to racism. *Currents*, vol. 1, no. 3, 24-25.

Ungerleider, C.S. (1985). Police Intercultural Education: Promoting Understanding and Empathy Between Police and Ethnic Communities. *Canadian Ethnic Studies*, 17, 1, 51-66.

6. GENERAL RESOURCES, BIBLIOGRAPHIES, CATALOGUES, AND PERIODICALS

Bancroft, G.W. (Ed.) (1976). *Outreach for Understanding: a Report on Intercultural Seminars*. Toronto: Ontario Ministry of Culture and Recreation.

Brilt, Margaret (Ed.) (1982). *Multiculturalism Film and Video Catalogue*. Canadian Film Institute, Ottawa.

Canada. *Publications Supported by the Multiculturalism Directorate*; Multiculturalism Canada, Ottawa, K1A 0M5.

Children's Book Centre. *Canadian Multicultural Books for Children*. 229 College Street, 5th floor, Toronto, Ontario, M5T 1R4.

Council on Interracial Books for Children. Racism/Sexism Resource Centre for Educators, 1841 Broadway, New York, New York 10023.

ERIC Clearinghouse on Elementary and Early Childhood Education. College of Education, University of Illinois, 1310 South Sixth Street, Champaign, Illinois, 61820.

Goldstein, J.E. and Bienvenue, R.M. (1980). *Ethnicity and Ethnic Relations in Canada*. Toronto; Butterworth and Co. Ltd.

Griffin, Louise. *Multi-ethnic Books for Young Children: Annotated Bibliography for Parents and Teachers*. National Association for the Education of Young Children, 1834 Connecticut Avenue, N.W., Washington, D.C. 20009.

Heritage Books and Treasures. Children's Culture Corner, 2551A Hurontario Street, Misissauga, Ontario, L5A 2G4.

Lee, Enid. (1984). *Tools for Resisting Racism in Canadian Schools: a Bibliography*. Toronto Metropolitan Separate School Board, Urban Alliance on Race Relations, 229 College Street, Toronto, Ontario, M5T 1R4.

Mallea, John R. and Shea, E.C. (1979). *Multiculturalism and Education: a Bibliography*. Toronto: The Ontario Institute for Studies in Education.

Markus, Roberta L. (1986). *Report on the Consultative Conference for Mutual Co-operation Between Toronto's Ryerson and Metropolitan Toronto's Culturally and Racially Diverse Community*. Toronto: Ryerson Press.

McLeod, Keith A. (Ed.) (1986-87). Multicultural education bibliographies for elementary schools, secondary schools and teachers. Prepared for the Canadian Teachers Federation. *Multiculturalism*, vol. 10, no. 2 & 3.

McNeil, E. and Schmidt, V. (1979). Cultural Awareness: A Resource Bibliography. Washington, D.C.: National Association for the Education of Young Children.

McNeil, E., Schmidt, V., and Allen, J. (1981). *Cultural Awareness for Young Children*. Texas: The Learning Tree.

Mock, K.R. (1986). Multicultural Early Childhood Education: an Annotated Bibliography and Resource List. Toronto: Masemann and Mock, 167 Ava Road, Toronto, Ontario, M6C 1W6.

Moodley, Kogila (Ed.) (1985). *Race relations and multicultural education.* Vancouver: Univertisy of British Columbia.

National Film Board of Canada Catalogue. McIntyre Educational Media Ltd., 30 Kelfield Street, Rexdale, Ontario, M9W 5A2.

Nova Scotia. Human Rights Commission (1984). *Textbook Analysis: Nova Scotia.* (UF 30) Halifax, 115.

Ontario. Ministry of Education (1977). *Multiculturalism in Action.* Toronto: the ministry.

Ontario. Ministry of Education (1988). A synopsis of public responses to the report of the Provincial Advisory Committee on Race Relations: the development of a policy on race and ethnocultural equity. Toronto: the ministry (Working Paper).

Ontario. Ministry of Education. *Race, Religion and Culture in Ontario School Materials: Suggestions for Authors and Publishers.* Toronto: the ministry.

Ontario. Ministry of Education and Ministry of Citizenship and Culture (1976). *Resource List for a Multicultural Society.* Toronto: the ministries. Available from Publications Ontario, 5th Floor, 880 Bay Street, Toronto, Ontario, M5A 1N8.

Pratt, D. (1984) Bias in Textbooks: Progress and Problems. In R. Samuda et al. (Eds.), *Multiculturalism in Canada: Social and Educational Perspectives.* Toronto: Allyn and Bacon, 154-166.

Ray, Douglas (1983). Human rights in education. *Multiculturalism*, vol. 6, no. 2, 5-7.

Ray, Douglas and D'Oyley, Vincent (Eds.) (1983). *Human Rights in Canadian Education.* Dubuque, Iowa: Kendall/Hunt Publishing Company.

Samuda, R.J., Berry, J.W. and Laferrière, M. (1984). *Multiculturalism in Canada: Social and Educational Perspectives.* Boston: Allyn and Bacon Inc.

Saskatchewan. Human Rights Commission (n.d.). *Prejudice in School Studies Textbooks: a Content Analysis of Social Studies Textbooks Used in Saskatchewan Schools.* Regina: the Commission 61.

Third World Books and Crafts Inc., 942 Bathurst Street, Toronto, Ontario, M5R 3G5.

TVOntario Video Resources Catalogue: Human Growth and Learning. TVOntario, Box 200, Station Q, Toronto, Ontario, M4T 2T1.

Wall, Naomi (1979). *Children's Books for Learning: A Bibliography of Multiethnic Resources for Classroom Use.* The Cross-Cultural Communication Centre, Toronto.

Yip, Gladys (1940). *Cross-cultural childrearing: an annotated bibliography.* Early Childhood Series, Centre for Curriculum and Instruction, University of British Columbia, Vancouver, B.C., V6T 1Z5.

Periodicals

Canadian and International Education. The Journal of the Comparative and International Education Society of Canada, Faculty of Education, University of Calgary, T2N 1N4.

Canadian Ethnic Studies. Calgary: University of Calgary Research Centre for Canadian Ethnic Studies, published semi-annually.

Canadian Children. Journal of the Canadian Association for Young Children, University of Calgary Press, 2500 University Drive, N.W., Calgary, Alberta, T2N 1N4. Special issue on multiculturalism, Vol. 10, 1986.

Cultures Canada. Multiculturalism Sector, Secretary of State, Ottawa, Ontario, K1A 0M5.

The History and Social Science Teacher, Faculty of Education, 1137 Western Road, London, Ontario, N6G 1G7.
(Note two special issues on multiculturalism: vol. 17, no. 1, 1981; and vol. 19, no. 2, 1983).

Multiculturalism, Faculty of Education, University of Toronto, 371 Bloor Street West, Toronto, Ontario, M5S 2R7.
Contains up-to-date articles and serves as a Bulletin for Canadian Council for Multicultural and Intercultural Education with nation-wide coverage of relevant issues and events.

Multicultural Teaching: To Combat Racism in School and Community (1989). Gillian Klein (Ed.), vol. 7, no. 2, spring. Published by Trentham Books, 151 Etrusia Road, Stoke-on-Trent, Staffordshire, ST1 5N5, England.

DEALING WITH RACIAL INCIDENTS AND DISCRIMINATION: AN ANNOTATED BIBLIOGRAPHY

Aboud, Frances (1988). *Children and prejudice.* New York: Basil Blackwell Inc.
Includes a note to educators on interethnic conflict among children ages 7-12 and suggests activities for fifth grade students to help reduce prejudicial attitudes.

Committee on Community, Race & Ethnic Relations, City of North York (1984). *Handling of racial/ethnic incidents in educational institutions.* North York, Ontario.
Resource kit to improve assistance and guidance in the handling of racial/ethnic incidents in schools. Will help with the development of policies and procedures as well as giving a suggested model for recording of racial and ethnic incidents.

Da Costa, G.A. (1978). Orphans and outlaws: some impacts of racism. *Multiculturalism,* vol. 11, no. 1.
Presents vignettes drawn from actual referrals for psychiatric evaluation as a result of "aggressive and disruptive" behavior, falling grades, or labelled as troublemaker at school. Gives some insight into the process of alienation and the effects on the adolescent.

Des Rivieres, Dennis (1984). Guidelines to assist in dealing with racial or ethnic incidents. *Currents: Readings in Race Relations.* Toronto: Urban Alliance on Race Relations, vol. 2, no. 3, 30-31.
Describes the pamphlet of the same name, which is part of the Metropolitan Separate School Board's Policy on Race Relations. In-service sessions with all board employees with this pamphlet were held over a two-year period to ensure that people would be ready to deal with the complexities of racial incidents.

Dreidger, Leo and Mezoff, Richard A. (1981). Ethnic prejudice and discrimination in Winnipeg high schools. *Canadian Journal of Sociology.* Edmonton: University of Alberta, vol. 6, no. 1, 1-16.
The author studied the ethnic prejudice and discrimination of high school (Grades 9-12) students in Winnipeg to evaluate the extent of: (1) differential treatment (2) prejudicial treatment (3) denial of desire and (4) disadvantaging treatment. A minority of students were generally inclined toward ethnic prejudice, while some others indicated prejudice toward select groups. Finding the meaning and defining the situation in which ethnic prejudice and discrimination takes place is a major concern of the researchers.

Goldring, Rolly (1982). *Race relations: studies in success - a multicultural high school - the l'Amoreaux experience.* Scarborough: Board of Education.

Elliston, Inez (1977). *Racial attitudes and racial violence in the school and school community in Metropolitan Toronto, Ontario. A survey of the opinion of personnel.* Scarborough: Board of Education.
Study concerning incidents of racism and racial attitudes in the school system, with some suggestions for dealing with evidence. Administrators, teachers, secretarial staff, and custodial staff were surveyed with regards to discrimination and violence and solutions for combatting racial attitudes. Recommendations for curriculum, teacher training, and handling of incidents is included.

Mallick, Heather (1987). Black picture. Racism still exists in schools, report says. Toronto: *The Globe and Mail*, July 10.
    Explores the possibility that blacks are sent into basic-level courses as a discrimination practice rather than any other criteria such as learning problems. Cites specific incidents of discrimination, but they are not legitimized within the school system. Gives an overview on the report by The Toronto Board of Education on how black students are faring.

Metropolitan Separate Schools (1984). *Guidelines to Assist in Dealing with Racial or Ethnic Incidents*. Toronto: Metropolitan Separate School Board.

Roe, M. (1982). *Multiculturalism, Racism and the Classroom*. Toronto: Canadian Education Association.

Task Force on Human Relations. Walter Pitman (Chairman) (1977). The long view: Metro's schools. *Now is Not Too Late*. Submitted to the Council of Metropolitan Toronto.
    Paper on race and violence in Metro. Chapter 5 deals with racism in Metro's schools. Although specific incidents are not cited, the information regarding administrative, staff roles and attitudes and curriculum development in reversing racial tensions in education is important. Also offers some suggestions for meeting the needs of minority groups within schools.

Thornhill, Esmeralda (1984). Fight Racism Starting With the Schools. *Currents*, vol. 2, no. 3, fall.

Toronto Board of Education (1979). Racial incidents in the schools. Some cases in point form the final report of the subcommitte on race relations. Section 4.
    Cites cases of actual racial incidents and how they were handled. Offers some solutions for school action and finishes with recommendations approved by the board.

APPENDIX A

LISTS OF BOARDS THAT PARTICIPATED IN THIS STUDY

APPENDIX A1

ALPHABETICAL LIST OF BOARDS IN SURVEY I

	PUBLIC		SEPARATE
1.	East York	1.	London and Middlesex County
2.	Etobicoke		
3.	Hamilton		
4.	Hearst	2.	Metropolitan Toronto
5.	Huron County		
6.	Lambton County	3.	Timmins District
7.	North York		
8.	Ottawa		
9.	Scarborough		
10.	Timiskaming		
11.	Timmins		
12.	Toronto		
13.	Waterloo		
14.	West Parry Sound		
15.	Windsor		
16.	York (City)		
17.	York Region		

APPENDIX A2

ALPHABETICAL LIST OF BOARDS THAT HAVE AN OVERALL POLICY
(Note 3 Drafts)

1. Brant County RCSSB
2. Bruce-Grey County RCSSB
3. Carleton RCSSB
4. Cochrane Iroquois Falls-Black River Matheson Board of Education (Draft)
5. Dufferin-Peel RCSSB
6. Durham Board of Education
7. Durham Region RCSSB
8. East York, Board of Education for the Borough of
9. Elgin County Board of Education (Draft)
10. Essex County RCSSB
11. Etobicoke, Board of Education for the City of
12. Frontenac County Board of Education
13. Frontenac-Lennox and Addington County RCSSB
14. Hamilton, Board of Education for the City of
15. Huron County Board of Education
16. Huron-Perth County RCSSB
17. Kirkland Lake Board of Education
18. Lakehead District RCSSB (Administrative Policy)
19. Lambton County Board of Education
20. London, Board of Education for the City of
21. London and Middlesex County RCSSB
22. Metropolitan Separate School Board
23. Nipigon-Red Rock Board of Education
24. North York, Board of Education for the City of
25. Ottawa Board of Education
26. Peel Board of Education
27. Scarborough, Board of Education for the City of
28. Stormont Dundas and Glengarry County Board of Education
29. Timiskaming Board of Education
30. Timiskaming District RCSSB
31. Timmins Board of Education
32. Timmins District RCSSB (French)
33. Toronto, Board of Education for the City of
34. Victoria County Board of Education
35. Waterloo County Board of Education
36. Waterloo Region RCSSB (Draft)
37. West Parry Sound Board of Education
38. Windsor, Board of Education for the City of
39. Windsor RCSSB
40. York, Board of Education for the City of
41. York Region RCSSB

APPENDIX A3

ALPHABETICAL LIST OF BOARDS THAT ARE DEVELOPING A POLICY

1. Carleton Board of Education
2. Essex County Board of Education
3. Halton Board of Education
4. Halton RCSSB
5. Hamilton-Wentworth RCSSB
6. Kenora Board of Education
7. Kent County Board of Education
8. Kent County RCSSB
9. Lake Superior Board of Education
10. Lakehead Board of Education
11. Leeds and Grenville County Board of Education
12. Manitoulin Board of Education
13. Middlesex County Board of Education
14. Niagara South Board of Education
15. Ottawa RCSSB
16. Oxford County Board of Education
17. Perth County Board of Education
18. Simcoe County RCSSB
19. Sudbury Board of Education
20. Welland County RCSSB
21. Wellington County Board of Education
22. York Region Board of Education

APPENDIX A4

ALPHABETICAL LIST OF BOARDS THAT DO NOT HAVE AN OVERALL POLICY

1. Brant County Board of Education
2. Bruce County Board of Education
3. Central Algoma Board of Education
4. Cochrane Iroquois Falls-Black River Matheson District RCSSB (French)
5. Conseil scolaire de langue française d'Ottawa-Carleton (French)
6. Dryden District RCSSB
7. East Parry Sound Board of Education
8. Espanola Board of Education
9. Fort Frances-Rainy River Board of Education
10. Geraldton Board of Education
11. Geraldton District RCSSB
12. Haldimand Board of Education
13. Haldimand-Norfolk RCSSB
14. Haliburton County Board of Education
15. Hastings County Board of Education
16. Hastings-Prince Edward County RCSSB
17. Kapuskasing District RCSSB (French)
18. Lambton County RCSSB
19. Lanark Leeds and Grenville County RCSSB
20. Lennox and Addington County Board of Education
21. Lincoln County RCSSB
22. Metropolitan Toronto School Board
23. Michipicoten Board of Education
24. Nipissing Board of Education
25. Nipissing District RCSSB
26. Norfolk Board of Education
27. North of Superior District RCSSB
28. North Shore Board of Education
29. North Shore District RCSSB
30. Northumberland and Newcastle Board of Education
31. Peterborough County Board of Education
32. Peterborough-Victoria-Northumberland and Newcastle RCSSB
33. Prince Edward County Board of Education
34. Red Lake Board of Education
35. Sault Ste. Marie Board of Education
36. Sault Ste. Marie District RCSSB
37. Simcoe County Board of Education

APPENDIX B

RESEARCH TOOLS

MASEMANN AND MOCK
Consultants in the Social Sciences

167 Ava Road
Toronto, Canada M6C 1W6
(416) 782-1050
(416) 922-4819

February 15, 1989

Dear

    We have been awarded a contract by the Ministry of Education to gather information on policy development in "race and ethnocultural equity in education". We are working with Dr. Mavis Burke to gather documentation, review the literature, and conduct interviews with key personnel in the various regions of Ontario.
    The purpose of this initial letter is to ask your co-operation in supplying two (2) copies of all the policy documents, administration documents, and support materials your Board has produced which pertain to race relations, multiculturalism, human rights, and/or equity. Since this is a short-term project with narrow time margins, we would appreciate receiving this documentation as close to February 28 as possible.
    Thank you very much for your assistance in this matter.

Yours sincerely,

Karen R. Mock Ph.D.
Principal Investigator

February 28, 1989

MASEMANN AND MOCK
Consultants in the Social Sciences

167 Ava Road
Toronto, Canada M6C 1W6
(416) 782-1050
(416) 922-4819

Dear

We have been awarded a contract by the Ministry of Education to gather information on policy development in "race and ethnocultural equity in education". While this is not a province-wide review, it is an attempt to gather as much information as possible from Boards of Education which may already have a policy, which may be in the process of developing policy, or which may deal with these issues in administrative documents.

We are working with Dr. Mavis Burke who is Special Advisor on Race Relations to Dr. Bernard Shapiro. We are sending the attached questionnaire to all Boards of Education in the province to ascertain what is the current state of policy development in race and ethnocultural equity and closely related areas. We realize that there are wide differences between Boards in policy development, and we would like an accurate picture of the current situation.

As well as information about progress in policy development and factors leading to success, we are also trying to ascertain what barriers and realities of life exist that make it difficult for policies to develop. Therefore, please do not interpret lack of development in a necessarily negative light. It is important to know why some Boards may have chosen other emphases.

We are asking for your co-operation in filling out this questionnaire **before March Break**, since our report is due at the end of the fiscal year. In addition, if you are willing to identify any key person who would like to talk to us about the process of policy development in your Board, please let us know their name and telephone number.

Thank you very much for your assistance in this project.

Yours sincerely,

Karen R. Mock

Karen R. Mock, Ph.D.
Principal Investigator

Encl.

lck

RACE AND ETHNOCULTURAL EQUITY POLICIES
IN ONTARIO SCHOOL BOARDS

QUESTIONNAIRE

Introduction

The purpose of this questionnaire is to ascertain how many school boards in Ontario have developed or are developing policies in ethnocultural and racial equity. It is also designed to survey your perceptions of the factors that help or hinder such a process, and the particular conditions that face your Board. The questions have been designed for speed of completion.

Questions   Name of Board _____

1. Does your Board of Education have written policy documents that pertain to racial and ethnocultural equity in your Board and schools?

    Yes _____

    No _____

    If you have not already sent them to us, would you please forward two (2) copies of any such policy documents, administrative documents, and support materials? Thank you.

2. Do you have policies or procedures that relate to other closely linked areas, such as the following:

    _____ a) multi-racial and anti-racist curriculum
    _____ b) heritage language
    _____ c) school and community relations
    _____ d) testing and assessment of non-English or non-French speakers
    _____ e) documentation of incidents of racial harassment
    _____ f) native studies
    _____ g) personnel policies and practices, e.g., employment equity
    _____ h) staff development
    _____ i) support services in guidance
    _____ j) other; please specify

    If they are relevant to racial and ethnocultural equity, could you please forward to us two (2) copies of any such documents or materials? Thank you.

RACE AND ETHNOCULTURAL EQUITY POLICIES
IN ONTARIO SCHOOL BOARDS

QUESTIONNAIRE

Introduction

The purpose of this questionnaire is to ascertain how many school boards in Ontario have developed or are developing policies in ethnocultural and racial equity. It is also designed to survey your perceptions of the factors that help or hinder such a process, and the particular conditions that face your Board. The questions have been designed for speed of completion.

Questions   Name of Board _____

1. Does your Board of Education have written policy documents that pertain to racial and ethnocultural equity in your Board and schools?

    Yes _____

    No _____

    If you have not already sent them to us, would you please forward two (2) copies of any such policy documents, administrative documents, and support materials? Thank you.

2. Do you have policies or procedures that relate to other closely linked areas, such as the following:

    _____ a) multi-racial and anti-racist curriculum
    _____ b) heritage language
    _____ c) school and community relations
    _____ d) testing and assessment of non-English or non-French speakers
    _____ e) documentation of incidents of racial harassment
    _____ f) native studies
    _____ g) personnel policies and practices, e.g., employment equity
    _____ h) staff development
    _____ i) support services in guidance
    _____ j) other; please specify

    If they are relevant to racial and ethnocultural equity, could you please forward to us two (2) copies of any such documents or materials? Thank you.

QUESTIONNAIRE
Page 2

3(a) Did your Board participate in the process of validation of the Ministry of Education document "The Development of a Policy on Race and Ethnocultural Equity"?

No _____

Yes _____

(b) If the answer was "yes", what was the follow-up to this process in your Board?

_____

_____

4. In terms of a subjective evaluation of your Board's process, please evaluate how far your Board is along the way to developing a policy. Check <u>one only</u>.

_____ We have a fully developed policy that is being implemented within our system.

_____ We have a fully developed policy that is at the early stages of implementation.

_____ We have an official policy, but there are few signs that it is being implemented.

_____ We are in the last stages of developing a policy.

_____ We are part-way through the process of developing a policy.

_____ We are in the early stages of developing a policy.

_____ We have various aspects of racial and ethnocultural equity policy embedded in many policy areas in our Board. We do not see it as an area separate and distinct on its own.

_____ None of the above statements apply to our situation. Our situation is the following: _____

_____

_____

_____

QUESTIONNAIRE
Page 3

5. What are the main racial and ethnocultural minority groups in the area served by your Board? List in order of magnitude.

   1. Most numerous _____

   2. _____

   3. _____

   4. _____

6. If you have a policy or are developing one, please describe briefly the process and the personnel involved in this process. Use an additional page if necessary.

   _____
   _____
   _____

7a) What do you think are the main factors that led to success in the development of your Board's policy?

   _____
   _____
   _____

OR

b) What do you think are the main factors that prevent success or are a barrier to policy development in this area in your Board?

   _____
   _____
   _____

QUESTIONNAIRE
Page 4

8. Are there any unique factors in your Board that would have to be taken into consideration in policy development of this type? (e.g., nature of school population, distance, existence of particular institutions or geographic features.)

_____

_____

_____

9. What local resources exist in your area that have been or could have been used in policy development and for professional development days in relation to racial and ethnocultural equity?

Human resources _____

Other resources _____

10. What do you see as your Board's highest priority in the next five years

   a) In matters of racial and ethnocultural equity?

   _____

   b) In general?

   _____

Thank you very much for answering this questionnaire. If you have a fully developed policy document, we would be interested in interviewing a key person in its development. We would appreciate your identifying such a person for us here.

Name _____ Telephone number _____

Title _____

Please return as soon as possible to:

   Masemann and Mock, Consultants
   167 Ava Road
   Toronto, Ontario
   M6C 1W6

Le 28 février 1989

MASEMANN AND MOCK
Consultants in the Social Sciences

167 Ava Road
Toronto, Canada M6C 1W6
(416) 782-1050
(416) 922-4819

Monsieur,

Le ministre de l'Éducation nous a accordé un contrat afin de recueillir de l'information sur le développement d'une politique en «équité raciale et ethnoculturelle». Bien qu'il ne s'agisse pas proprement dit d'une enquête provinciale, il s'agit d'un effort visant à rassembler le plus de renseignements possible sur les conseils scolaires qui, déjà, peuvent avoir une telle politique, qui sont en train d'en développer une ou qui pourraient traiter de ces questions dans des documents administratifs.

Nous travaillons avec Mme Mavis Burke qui est conseillère spéciale en relations raciales auprés du M. Bernard Shapiro. Nous faisons parvenir le questionnaire ci-joint à tous les conseils scolaires de la province afin de vérifier l'état actuel de développement d'une politique en éthique raciale et ethnoculturelle ainsi que de champs connexes. Nous réalisons qu'il peut exister de vastes différences entre les conseils pour ce qui est du développement d'une telle politique et nous aimerions pouvoir dégager une image précise de la situation courante.

Outre la cueillette de l'information concernant les progrès réalisés dans l'établissement d'une politique ainsi que des facteurs qui ont mené à son succès, nous essayons aussi d'évaluer quels obstacles et réalités quotidiennes existent qui peuvent rendre difficile sa réalisation. Par conséquent, il ne faudrait pas nécessairement interpréter un manque de développement dans une lumière négative. Il nous est important de comprendre pourquoi quelques conseils pourraient avoir choisi de mettre l'accent ailleurs.

Le 28 février 1989
Page 2

Nous vous demandons votre collaboration afin de remplir ce questionnaire avant le 21 mars étant donné que notre rapport arrive à échéance à la fin de l'exercice financier. De plus, si vous désirez identifier une personne-clé qui aimerait s'entretenir avec nous sur le processus de développement d'une politique à l'intérieur de votre conseil, s.v.p., faites-nous connaître ses nom et numéro de téléphone. Si vous avez la moindre question, s.v.p., n'hésitez pas à contacter notre assistante à la recherche, Mme Jacinthe Fraser au numéro (416) 978-7836 ou 465-2158.

Je vous remercie de votre appui et vous prie d'agréer, monsieur, l'éxpression de mes sentiments les meilleurs.

Karen R. Mock

Karen R. Mock, Ph.D.
Chercheure principale

POLITIQUES D'ÉQUITE RACIALE ET ETHNOCULTURELLE
DANS LES CONSEILE SCOLAIRES DE L'ONTARIO

QUESTIONNAIRE

Introduction

Le but de ce questionnaire est de vérifier combien de conseils scolaires en Ontario ont développé ou sont en train de développer des politiques d'éthique raciale et ethnoculturelle. Il se propose aussi d'examiner vos perceptions quant aux facteurs qui pourraient aider ou nuire au processus et veut évaluer les conditions particulières auxquelles fait face votre conseil. Les questions ont été conçues pour faciliter la rapidité d'exécution.

Questions   Nom du conseil

1. Votre conseil scolaire posséde-t-il des documents écrits rattachés à une politique d'équité raciale et ethnoculturelle dans votre conseil ou vos écoles?

    Oui

    Non

    Si vous ne l'avez pas fait déjà, voudriez-vous s.v.p. nous envoyer deux (2) copies de ces documents ainsi que des documents administratifs ou matériaux de soutien s'y rapportant? Merci.

2. Avez-vous des politiques ou des procédures qui rattachent à des champs connexes telsque les suivants :

    a) programmes multi-raciaux et anti-racistes
    b) langues ancestrales
    c) écoles et relations communautaires
    d) mesures et évaluation des allophones (ne parlant ni français ni anglais)
    e) documentation d'incidents d'harcèlement racial
    f) études autochtones
    g) politiques et pratiques concernant le personnel (ex., équité d'embauche)
    h) développement du personnel
    i) services de soutien en orientation
    j) autre; s.v.p., précisez

    S'ils relèvent de l'équité raciale et ethnoculturelle, voudriez-vous nous faire parvenir deux (2) copies de tout document ou matériaux ainsi identifiés? Merci.

QUESTIONNAIRE
Page 2

3. (a) Votre conseil a-t-il participé au processus d'examen critique du document du ministère de l'Éducation «Le développement d'une politique d'équité raciale et ethnoculturelle»?

   Non

   Oui

   (b) Si la réponse était oui, quel a été le suivi à ce processus à l'intérieur de votre conseil?

4. Sous forme d'évaluation subjective de l'évolution de votre conseil, évaluez s.v.p. le chemin parcouru pour établir une politique. Identifiez une réponse seulement.

   Nous avons développé une politique complète laquelle est mise sur pied dans notre système

   Nous avons développé une politique complète qui en est aux premières étapes de mise sur pied

   Nous avons une politique officielle mais il y a peu de signes qu'elle soit mise sur pied

   Nous en sommes aux dernières étapes du développement d'une politique

   Nous sommes à mi-chemin dans le processus de développement d'une politique

   Nous en sommes aux premiers stages de développement d'une politique

   Nous avons des aspects variés d'une politique d'équité raciale et ethnoculturelle intégrés à d'autres politiques. Nous ne la percevons pas comme une politique séparée et distincte en soi

   Aucune des affirmations précédentes ne s'applique à notre situation. Notre situation est la suivante :

QUESTIONNAIRE
Page 3

5. Quels sont les principaux groupes minoritaires linguistiques, raciaux et ethnoculturels desservis par votre conseil? Dressez-en une liste par ordre d'importance.

   1. Les plus nombreux

   2.

   3.

   4.

6. Si vous avez une politique ou êtes en train d'en développer une, s.v.p., décrivez-en brièvement le processus d'évolution ainsi que le personnel qui s'y est impliqué. Ajoutez une page si nécessaire.

7. (a) Quels sont croyez-vous les principaux facteurs qui ont mené au succès quant au développement de la politique de votre conseil?

OU

   (b) Quels sont croyez-vous les principaux facteurs qui empêchent le succès ou qui s'avèrent des obstacles au développement d'une politique dans le domaine à l'intérieur de votre conseil?

QUESTIONNAIRE
Page 4

8. Y a-t-il des facteurs uniques à votre conseil et qui devraient être pris en considération an niveau du développement d'une politique de ce type? (par ex., nature de la clientele estudiantine, distance, existence d'institutions ou d'aspects géographiques particuliers.)

9. Quelles ressources locales ont été ou auraient pu être utilisées dans l'établissement d'une politique ainsi que de journées pédagogiques visant l'équité raciale et ethnoculturelle?

   Ressources humaines

   Autres ressources

10. Que voyez-vous comme étant la plus grande priorité pour votre conseil pendant les prochaines cinq années?

    a) En matiere d'équité raciale et ethnoculturelle?

    b) En général?

Merci de vous avoir prêté à ce questionnaire. Si vous avez finalisé un document concernant votre politique, nous serions intéressées à interviewer une personne qui a joué un rôle-clé dans la réalisation de ce document. Nous aimerions que vous puissiez identifier ici une telle personne.

Nom   Numéro de téléphone

Titre

S.v.p., retournez aussitôt que possible à :

   Masemann et Mock, Conseillères
   167 Ava Road
   Toronto, Ontario
   M6C 1W6

SURVEY OF RACIAL AND ETHNOCULTURAL EQUITY POLICIES

Questions for Interviews.

I. Policy Development

1. When did the process of policy development begin at your board?

   Started ------------------------------------

   Completed ----------------------------------

   How long? ----------------------------------

2. What was the catalyst for policy development?

3. How did the board go about beginning the process?

4. What was the composition of the committee/task force? Size? Structure? Chair? Reporting to?

5. What was the role of the community in policy a) development b) validation c) implementation?

6. What resources were used? internal/board/local/other?

7. How would you describe the student population of the board geographically? urban/rural, large/medium/small?

8. How would you describe the student population of the board re: demographics/recent changes?

9. How does this policy compare with other policies in the board? Process/structure/physical appearance/implementation process/accountability?

10. What in your opinion were the key factors in the success of policy development in the area of multicultural/race relations?

11. Other comments on the policy development phase.

II. Implementation.

1. Was there a specific implementation plan developed at the time of the policy? Time lines/administrative procedures/evaluation?

2. How far would you say the implementation has progressed?

3. How would you describe the implementation of this policy? How is it going? How would you evaluate the results? Any research? Behaviour? Incidents?

4. What would you say were the barriers to the specific implementation of such policies?

5. Can you identify key factors in successful policy implementation?

6. Any other comments?

19 April 1988

Dear

We are writing with reference to the recent letter and questionnaire we sent concerning policies on race and ethnocultural equity. We are very grateful to the 74 Boards which have responded to the questionnaire and which have sent copies of their policies. To all of you who responded in March, we send our sincere thanks.

The other purpose of this letter is to inform you about the follow-up phase and interviewing process. The response to our questionnaire was so thorough that we have had to limit interviewing to Boards in each region which have fully developed policies. The deadline for this project is still a very short one and we regret we are not able to interview people from every Board; however, the material we have received from all Boards is extremely useful and will be summarized in the final report.

For those of you who have still not responded, we would appreciate your filling in the attached sheet very quickly, so that we can reduce the number of "No Response" answers in the final statistics. We assume that Boards which have not replied are probably in the "No Policy" category, but it is important for you to confirm this.

At this point, the policies have been collected into binders and the tabulations of the questionnaires are almost complete. The interviewing phase will be completed in the next few weeks.

Once again, many thanks for your co-operation in this study.

Yours sincerely,

Karen R. Mock

Karen R. Mock, Ph.D.
Principal Investigator

lck

19 April 1989

FOR NON-RESPONDENTS ONLY

Follow-up to Questionnaire on Racial and Ethnocultural Equity

1. Name of Board _____

2. Does your Board have an overall policy on racial and ethnocultural equity?

    YES _____   NO _____

3. Does your Board have any support documentation or administrative procedures referring to related areas such as curriculum, personnel policies, or racial harassment?

    YES _____   NO _____

We would appreciate receiving two (2) copies of any policies or documentation if it is available. Thank you very much for completing this follow-up sheet.

Karen R. Mock

Karen Mock, Ph.D.
Principal Investigator

MASEMANN AND MOCK
Consultants in the Social Sciences

167 Ava Road
Toronto, Canada M6C 1W6
(416) 782-1050
(416) 922-4819

May 11, 1989

Thank you very much for responding to our letters requesting information on policies of racial and ethnocultural equity. We sincerely regret any misunderstanding our recent letter may have caused, as the follow-up questionnaire was meant only for Boards that had previously not responded.

We are working on assembling all of the policies in a format that is easily accessible by all Boards, and further information will be sent to you when it is available.

Once again, many thanks for your participation in this study.

Yours sincerely,

Karen Mock

Karen R. Mock, Ph.D.
Principal Investigator

lck

Le 8 juin 1989

MASEMANN AND MOCK
Consultants in the Social Sciences

167 Ava Road
Toronto, Canada M6C 1W6
(416) 782-1050
(416) 922-4819

Monsieur le directeur,

Nous tenons par la présente à vous remercier d'avoir répondu à nos lettre et questionnaire demandant des informations sur votre politique d'équité raciale et ethnoculturelle.

Nous en sommes maintenant à rassembler toutes les politiques dans un document dont le format se veut d'accès facile à tous les conseils scolaires. Nous recommuniquerons avec vous aussitôt que ce document sera disponible.

Pour le moment, ces politiques sont surtout en anglais.

Nous vous réitérons nos remerciements, nous rappelant aussi tous ceux ou celles qui ont participé à une entrevue téléphonique ou nous ont autrement fait connaître leur situation.

Sincèrement vôtre,

Jacinthe Fraser
    pour
Masemann et Mock,
Conseillères

jf